HAIDA GWAII LESSON

A
**Strategic Playbook
for Indigenous
Sovereignty**

MARK DOWIE

Illustrations by
April Sgaana Jaad White

Published by Inkshares, Inc., San Francisco, California
www.inkshares.com

Edited by Jennifer Sahn & Jessica Gardner
Cover design by CoverKitchen | Illustrated by April Sgaana Jaad White |
Interior design by Kevin G. Summers

ISBN: 9781942645559
e-ISBN: 9781942645566
Library of Congress Control Number: 2017940694

First edition

Printed in the United States of America

For

The Siwanoy

TABLE OF CONTENTS

PREFACE

Why This Book and Why Now

I DECIDED to write this book while researching its predecessor, *Conservation Refugees*, an investigative history of the hundred-year conflict between global conservation and native peoples. Quite frequently, in remote communities around the world, a shaman, elder, or chief would ask me, "Do you know the Haida?"

I had heard of the Haida and seen their remarkable art in museums. But that was about it. "Why do you ask?" I would respond. "Because we want what they have" was the general response. And by that it turned out they meant "aboriginal title," a form of land tenure that gives indigenous occupants of a traditional homeland final say over who lives there, who is and is not a citizen of that land, and how and by whom resources will be extracted and used.

How did a small remote band of seafaring aboriginals who had lived for millennia on a remote archipelago in the north

Pacific get all those things back from a British colony that had usurped them, one by one, in the eighteenth century?

This book is the answer to that question. It's not a simple answer—though I have tried to make it as clear and understandable as possible—but neither was it an easy path for the Haida. It took them fifty years of political strategizing, legal maneuvering, alliance building, information gathering, public campaigning, blockading, media manipulation, land-use planning, and astute negotiation—alongside long hours of self-examination, deliberation, historical reassessment, debating, careful planning, and finding common cause with rivals. Still, for the Haida, the struggle ain't over yet, though they're a lot closer to their goals than most other indigenous communities around the world. Their story is not only a lesson; it's an inspiring tale of resilience and determination in the face of two centuries of persistent rudeness, oppression, and exploitation.

* * *

THERE IS an endless debate among historians, anthropologists, journalists, and indigenous peoples about what to call the original inhabitants of the New World. *Indian* is insulting to some, as are *Indio* and *Amerindian*. The main problem with *Indian* is that it overlooks the enormous diversity and ignores the true names and wildly differing cultures of Native Americans on two continents. *Native* has been co-opted by nativists. *Aboriginal* tends to identify Australian natives, although the definition of *aboriginal* (literally, "from the origin") pretty much describes First Peoples everywhere, and is used quite frequently in international law.

Indigenous peoples seems to offend no one, but is rarely used for self-description of specific "tribes" or "tribals." (I've lost count of how many times I've been asked not to use those terms.)

Although it is almost exclusively a Canadian term, I use *First Nation(s)* when referring to indigenous communities around the world, because it describes pretty much any legitimate and sovereign nation that preexisted the arrival and occupation of European settlers. They were there first. Not all of them had laws, a constitution, or what we would today regard as a national government, but they all had land, bordered territories, and hunting grounds that, along with a culture, language, and distinct people, *they* defined as a "nation."

Another term I'll use a lot, because Canada does so in most of its legal proceedings, is *the Crown*. It can mean the state, the federal or provincial government, or (in early colonial history) the royal place at the capital of an empire, or it can literally mean the sovereign imperial monarch who wears the crown—George of Britain, Ferdinand of Spain, Louis of France, or Maria of Portugal. However it is defined, the Crown, as I use it, is the power with which First Nations have had to and still have to contend.

* * *

YOU WILL notice that I have used very few proper names in telling this story. That will seem strange to many readers, particularly those who enjoy reading about colorful personalities or have read enough Haida history to know that there were definite heroes, men and women who sacrificed much in their long battle for freedom and self-determination. But I have minimized using names and profiling heroes because the Haida are a profoundly modest and anti-narcissistic culture, and it's their story that the indigenous world wants to know—a story of collective leadership, not individual heroism; of patient determination, not celebrity biopics or amusing anecdotes about colorful elders, warriors, and hereditary chiefs. This does not mean that there aren't creative, selfless, tireless Haida leaders who have served faithfully in key positions of power. In fact, while traveling the islands and researching this book, I found some of the most remarkable people I have ever met.

But one of the characteristics that stood out for me about Haida leaders, men and women alike, is that they do not strive for reverence, fame, or name recognition. What they do, they do for their community, not just for themselves, their immediate family, or historical distinction. As one former Haida Council president observes, "Focusing on the individual is not the Haida way." OK, I'll tell you his name. It's Guujaaw, an affable, mischievous, humorous, and brilliant man, and a talented artist and drummer, who inspired and shepherded many of the decisive Haida battles of the past half century and served as president of the Haida Nation from 2000 to 2012. We had two long conversations while I was in Haida Gwaii, one sitting, one walking. I still have cramps in my right hand from taking notes.

Of course, the Haida are acutely aware of what Guujaaw and other leaders have accomplished, and those men and women are held in high esteem. But their goal is not fame. It is, in a word, independence, which they know is something that cannot be won by one or even a handful of people. It is won by a nation, as the story in this book attests.

What the Haida would like the world to know is what they have accomplished—the *how* of it, not the *who*. They know that what was said or written or done is more important and relevant to other indigenous peoples than their names and personal stories.

So I tell their story as a series of well-timed decisions and actions because it is those events, not the colorful individuals who designed, executed, or led them, that needs to be understood by native leaders around the world who asked that pressing question: "How did they do it?"

* * *

WHILE THE Haida created a strategy for self-determination that worked, there are scores, if not hundreds, of First Nations around the world for whom these tactics would not be appropriate, at least not yet. Their situations are so dire, so uncertain, and their oppressors so aggressive and potentially violent, that blockades and litigation would simply be futile, even dangerous.

However, there are hundreds, perhaps thousands, of indigenous communities—some larger, some smaller—that exist entirely under the sovereignty of a nation-state that absorbed them, without consultation, assuming complete tenure and title over their land and licensing its use and extraction of resources to anyone they please. It is for them this book is written.

INTRODUCTION

Whole nations melted away like balls of snow
before the sun.

Tsiyu Gansini[1]

ACCORDING TO the UN, there are 370 million self-described "indigenous peoples" alive today. Generally defined as people whose community preexisted a larger nation-state that enveloped them, indigenous peoples comprise about 4,500 distinct cultures and speak as many different languages and dialects. While making up only 5 percent of the world's total population, they occupy about 20 percent of the planet's land surface. They exist within and straddle the borders of 75 of the United Nations' 193 recognized countries.

They live in tropical forests, boreal forests, deserts, and snow, on tundra, savannas, prairies, islands, and mountains, and they occupy every remaining complex biotic community (or "biome") on the planet. They are stewards of about 80 percent of the world's remaining biological diversity and account for 90 percent of its cultural diversity.

1 (aka Dragging Canoe) Cherokee war chief

Many of them regard their ancestral territory as a nation—a First Nation—and would draw a very different map of the world than that found in most modern atlases. Instead of 193 "sovereign" countries, theirs would demarcate thousands of independent nations.

For most of the millennia they have endured, these small nations knew little of each other's existence, languages, cultures, or lifeways. Nevertheless, they have somehow managed during the last century to cobble together one of the most remarkable worldwide social movements in the history of mankind, a movement to reassert their rights to self-determination and claims to the territories they have traditionally occupied.

An early indication of the movement was the small delegation of British Columbia Indian chiefs who traveled to London in 1906 to petition King Edward VII over the lack of treaties and the inadequacies of Indian reserves in their province. Similar petitions followed from other BC First Nations, including the Haida. While British authorities listened patiently and respectfully to the chiefs, the provincial government in Victoria, BC, stubbornly refused to recognize aboriginal title. However, in 1913, a Royal Commission on Indian Affairs was created by the Crown. For three years, commissioners listened to more claims and arguments for aboriginal title and sovereignty. The commission's conclusion, however, was that Canadian natives were "content and prosperous," and there was no systematic land problem.

The indigenous movement went global in 1923 when a Canadian Mohawk chief named Deskaheh led a small delegation of North American Indians to Geneva, Switzerland. There they called upon the recently formed League of Nations to defend the rights of their people to live under their own laws, on their own land, and according to their own faith. They were turned away at the gate and told that they were addressing a matter of domestic policy—"Go home and deal directly with your governments" (which of course they had been doing, to no avail, and was why they had gone to Geneva).

In the decades that followed, millions of very poor, almost illiterate people living in thousands of small communities, without electricity or communication infrastructure, and speaking thousands of different languages, managed to organize a global protest for land and human rights that has literally changed the way the world regards land tenure, the commons, human rights, and sovereignty.

As the world shrank due to telecommunications and transportation, inhabitants of the most remote villages began to discover that they were not alone. There were others like them on almost every continent—people with unique dialects, diets, cultures, and cosmologies who were at best misunderstood, at worst oppressed by the dominant nationalities that surrounded and subsumed them. They began to communicate, and to meet, and through interpreters learned of ways that aboriginals in societies like Haida Gwaii were finding to protect their cultures and recover the independence, culture, and ancient homelands lost to colonialism. They began to use terms like *self-determination*, resist assimilation, and petition provincial and national courts (and eventually the United Nations) for recognition of territorial and aboriginal rights.

And people in the "developed" world who valued cultural diversity as much as biological diversity—particularly anthropologists, human rights lawyers, social activists, and members of organizations like Cultural Survival, Survival International, EcoTerra, Amazon Watch, the Forest Peoples Programme, Terralingua, the International Forum on Indigenous Peoples, and First Peoples Worldwide—came to their aid. Links were established, networks formed, and new NGOs founded, from the Arctic to the Kalahari, from Micronesia to the Amazon basin, some with fewer than one hundred members, others with millions.

By 1960, indigenous peoples were formally petitioning national courts and governments, international bodies, and the World Bank to have their civil, economic, cultural, and land rights recognized, and for the right to self-determination. They had also begun to confront transnational extractive industries that were treating their homelands as if they were part of some distorted global commons available to any nation whose industry needed the resources above and below the ground.

On December 14, 1960, the Declaration on the Granting of Independence to Colonial Countries and Peoples was adopted by the United Nations General Assembly. It was a response to colonized countries and peoples' call for an end to colonization "in all its forms and manifestations." The declaration stated that "all people have the right to self-determination… to freely determine their political status and pursue their economic, social and cultural development."

While indigenous peoples were not specifically mentioned in the declaration, and few nations interpreted it to in any way include the thousands of small nations that had been colonized, Canada did allow its natives to pursue land claims, and gave them citizenship in 1965 and the right to vote in 1973.

As the 1960s and '70s unfolded, new and somewhat less polite tactics were tested by indigenous peoples—nonviolent direct action, passive resistance, labor strikes, public demonstrations, litigation, and boycotts. It was an era of disobedience and rebellion, when minorities' worldwide resistance to oppression and injustice was joined by the vibrant force of native people. Armed struggle became an option seriously considered by the oppressed, including leaders of the American Indian Movement and similar organizations around the world. The Haida, a ferocious warrior people, deliberated it briefly, but decided that nonviolent direct action, litigation, and negotiation offered the best path for them to reconciliation and sovereignty.

A turning point arrived in 1974 when indigenous leaders from North America, Latin America, Australia, and New Zealand established the World Council of Indigenous Peoples. It was immediately granted consultative status by the United Nations.

In 1977, Native Americans petitioned the Decolonization Committee of the United Nations for the following privileges:

- Recognition of their sovereign right to self-determination
- Full ownership of their communal lands
- Control of their natural wealth and resources
- Cultural freedom
- Informed consent prior to any activity on their lands
- Self-representation through their own institutions
- Freedom to exercise their customary laws

As the League of Nations had fifty years beforehand, the UN ignored the petition.

In the years that followed, indigenous communities like the Haida continued to challenge all the assumptions and mechanisms that resulted in the dispossession of their lands, one government and one court at a time. The global movement for native sovereignty called these groups "pockets of resistance." They have been more successful in some countries than others, particularly in Canada, where the Haida became an exemplar.

This book is the Haida's story, offered with full tribal cooperation, support, and encouragement, both for its author and for indigenous peoples worldwide struggling for their title, sovereignty, and independence.

I

The Place

*There is nowhere more beguiling, more hypnotic,
more intoxicating and infuriating and enigmatic, more
ineffable, than Haida Gwaii.*

Ian Gill

THERE IS something alluring about islands, each of them a small world unto itself. Remote and beckoning, they compel us to come ashore and stay awhile, explore their individuality, and contemplate life in the stream. Jam a hundred or so of them into a dense aquatic archipelago, and you have an irresistible magnet. The wild and lush islands of Haida Gwaii,[2] with their four thousand miles of shoreline punctuated by streams from eight hundred separate watersheds, are as alluring as any on Earth, particularly the smaller, isolated islets that have been given names like

---

2 The popular translation of Haida Gwaii is "Islands of the People." But that name is derived from "Xaaydlaa Gwaayaay," which translates literally from Xaayda Kil, the Haida language, as "Taken out of Concealment."

"Tuft," "Flatrock," "Monument," and (my personal favorite) "All Alone Stone."

When I first approached the eastern shoreline of the islands in the spring of 2015, I tried to imagine them being seen by humans for the first time. Were ancestors of the Haida as enthralled as I was, as drawn to their mossy intertidal flats, their impenetrable forests rising dramatically to the distant snowcapped San Cristobal Mountains? The place seemed so inviting, so pure and peaceful, until days later when I saw the islands from the other side.

Most of the western shoreline of Haida Gwaii lies at the edge of the continental shelf—an abrupt tectonic scarp rising from nine thousand feet below sea level to the three-thousand-foot peaks of the San Cristobals. The rocky and treacherous coastline is pounded day after day by waves as high as ninety feet, pushed shoreward by violent Pacific storms featuring winds up to one hundred miles an hour. There are few other places on the planet with shorelines as hostile to man and nature. Together, wave and wind toss huge boulders and massive driftwood timbers over tall bluffs, smashing them into spruce forests that have somehow survived centuries of bombardment.

About twenty million years ago, this 3,700-square-mile chunk of volcanic rock broke off from the North American mainland and drifted over countless millennia to the edge of the Pacific continental shelf, where it remains today, resting perilously along the converging Pacific and North American Plates. The islands sit directly over one of the planet's most seismically active faults, known affectionately as "the Charlotte," which produces a memorable earthquake every thirty years or so.

The last of twenty or so Pleistocene glaciations began its retreat from the archipelago around 16,000 BCE, about two thousand years earlier than the rest of the North American glacial masses. The retreat ended about thirteen thousand years ago, the same time that humans first appeared on the islands. Because of the way the place was covered with ice, Haida Gwaii is regarded by nature historians as a "partial refugium," a refuge for plant and animal species that preexisted and survived the Ice Age—at least thirty-nine species, including rare or distinctive subspecies of the saw-whet owl, hairy woodpecker, Steller's jay, and Peale's peregrine falcon. Then there are the mammals, each unique in one way or another to Haida Gwaii, which claims its own strains of pine marten, river otter, Haida ermine, dusky shrew, silver-haired bat, Keen's myotis, little brown bat, deer mouse, and *Ursus americanus carlottae*, the largest black bear in the world. All

Haida Architecture

I have seen houses two hundred and twenty feet long, and thirty feet wide, built with much skill, and containing five or six hundred people.

Amerigo Vespucci (1502)

AFTER RESIDING on one of the most seismically active faults on the planet for a few thousand years, the Haida have learned to design and build structures to withstand the heaviest earthquakes the planet's tectonic plates have to offer. Their gable-roofed, two-beam rectangular houses, sheathed with wide hand-split planks, have held up under innumerable magnitude-eights, with no doubt more on the way.

The basic post-and-beam structure of their magnificent longhouses is augmented with a framework of light rafters, sills, corner posts, and gables, to which the plank sheathing is applied. There is little integration between the massive framing and the light wall covering—the house is all frame.

Traditional Haida longhouses had plank floors and a central excavated fire pit lined with retaining planks. Some even had an underground cellar for hunkering down in extremely cold weather. They had a round doorway that was built into the design of the front central totem pole that decorated every house. The gable roofs of wealthy houses were

of these species have adapted characteristics so different from their mainland counterparts that they are now regarded by wildlife biologists as endemic to Haida Gwaii; they exist only there, in a unique tapestry of life so varied and fecund that biologists have dubbed the islands "the Galapagos of the North." Add to those species a long list of strange plants and iridescent mosses found only on the archipelago, and you have a truly extraordinary setting—a visual, sonic stage so unique and bizarre in places that it could easily have been the set for *Avatar*.

Unfortunately, due to a century of heavy forestry inflicted on the islands by the government of British Columbia, the introduction of species like the Sitka black-tailed deer and the common raccoon, and the arrival of Norwegian rats on ships, several plants and animals are on the brink of extinction. Hunting and trapping have also taken their tolls. The Dawson caribou

(*Rangifer tarandus dawsoni*), once unique to Haida Gwaii and a vital source of protein for its only predator, humans, vanished long ago. So too did the sea otter, whose pelts once adorned royalty on every continent. The otters are slowly returning, and there is talk of introducing a small caribou genetically similar to *dawsoni*, but eighty more local plants and animals remain officially listed as "threatened."

It's hard to wander about Haida Gwaii today, fighting your way through one of the densest rainforests in the world, an ecosystem that by weight supports more biomass than any other on the planet, and imagine it without a single tree anywhere in sight. But it was that way even as it was first settled by humans, who evolved so closely for four or five thousand years with primeval conifers like the monumental Sitka spruce and the red cedar that the trees are almost regarded as blood relatives by the Haida today. "An indulgent

sheathed in wide planks, while those of commoners were covered in cedar bark.

Longhouses were distinguished by a single horizontal beam running the full width of the front and back facades of the house at the level of the eaves. Exterior wall planks ran both vertically above those beams and horizontally below them. The roof had a centrally located square hole framed by a plank shield for smoke emission from the household fire.

Western red cedar has always been their material of choice. With some notable exceptions, house facades were left unpainted. However, the interior posts and screens were often carved.

Sometime toward the end of the eighteenth century, the people of Haida Gwaii developed a second type of house construction that more effectively married the post-and-beam structure to the exterior walls and roof. This six-beam house integrates all of the structural members and distributes the loads by employing more elaborate joinery, including mortise-and-tenon joints and interlocking features. Joinery also further integrates the sheathing into the post-and-beam frame. Sometimes, wall planks were bent by steaming and forced to overlap, thus producing a weathertight wall. The six-beam system opened up the interior of the house, making its use more flexible, because interior free-standing house posts were no longer necessary.

Besides providing for column-free interior space, the extensive use of joinery in this type of house, with its structural supports

god could have provided nothing better," Haida master carver and canoe maker Bill Reid remarked of the cedar, his favorite medium and the botanical fountainhead of his culture.

Between the islands and the mainland lies Hecate Strait, a shallow body of water averaging about fifty miles between shores. Appropriately named after the Greek goddess of witchcraft and sorcery, and renamed "the black bitch" by local sailors, the strait is one of the most treacherous bodies of water on Earth. A combination of shallow water, strong currents, and high winds can change a flat calm into roiling twenty-foot chop in a matter of minutes. There's a lot of sea wreckage on its floor.

Before the Ice Age, a portion of the strait was exposed and a level grassy plain stretched at least halfway across it. In fact, it seems likely that at one point the islands may have briefly been accessible by foot from the mainland. Such a land bridge would explain the existence of black bears and other mainland species that couldn't possibly have evolved on or swum to the islands. In small valleys on the submerged plain, robotic submarines have also found convincing evidence of man-made fish weirs dating back 13,700 years.

The warm Japanese current swirls north from the equator and turns a climate that should be barely habitable into something akin to Scotland's, and which supports one of the most diverse marine ecosystems in the world. The constant upwelling of those nutrient-rich currents provides sustenance to one of the most productive wild fisheries on the planet, food stock not only for the human inhabitants of the islands, but also for the carnivorous salmon, huge colonies of seals and sea lions, over thirty species of whale, dolphins, porpoises, and millions of fish-eating birds. The diversity of intertidal life around the islands

integrated into the exterior walls, added structural strength. This new architecture was stimulated by trading with European seamen, which brought the Haida metal tools and exposure to European and maritime joinery.

Family crests and myths were portrayed on prominent doorway poles and the free-standing poles that rose before the buildings like proud genealogies. Dating the phases of Haida monumental art has prompted considerable speculation. Northwest coast art forms were firmly established before the influx of traders, metal tools, and European paints in the early 1800s, but the fur trade certainly increased their quantity and probably their quality.

draws marine biologists from every university in the world. And that's just the shoreline.

Inland, there are more endemic and disjunct species than have been found just about anywhere else on Earth... certainly more than the Galapagos. Birders will find a quarter million breeding pairs of seabirds and the world's largest concentration of Peale's peregrine falcons. Trumpeter swans and sandhill cranes take refuge in company with tufted puffins, Cassin's auklets, ancient murrelets, and Leach's storm petrels, all of them prey to the largest bald eagle concentration on the west coast.

Place is a factor in all struggles for human sovereignty, and a landmass bordered on all sides by water is a huge advantage for any peoples claiming title. The boundary is obvious and incontestable. And it's unlikely that, before "discovery" and/or "conquest," more than one community of people ever lived there. Geography provided one of the Haida's great advantages in their struggle for independence: their land has been theirs forever. Their claim, therefore, seems clear to them.

To the shared amazement of biologists and anthropologists, nomadic humans have managed to find and thrive on some of the most challenging and hostile places on Earth. Haida Gwaii is high on their list of unlikely places for sustained human settlement. And the Haida Nation are near the top of almost every anthropologist's list of exceptional civilizations. Every community in the world seems to excel at something; to thrive and create the culture they did on Haida Gwaii, the Haida have really had to excel at almost everything.

2

The People

We do not inherit the earth from our ancestors,
we borrow it from our children.

Haida wisdom[3]

EVERY CULTURE has at least two origin stories, its own and
the one presumed by anthropologists. Sometimes historians alter
one story or the other, or tell a completely different story altogether. And of course, religions complicate the issue by injecting their
own cosmologies and eschatologies.

Indigenous peoples generally prefer and embrace their own
creation stories, the ones passed orally from generation to generation, about how they originated (not arrived from somewhere
else) in their ancient homelands, thousands or even millions
of years ago. Many of these communities refer to themselves as

---

3 No one seems to know the true origin of this sentiment. The Haida do not claim to have said it first, but they
embrace it as part of the worldview and wisdom they pass along to their children, as do many other First Nations of
the world.

simply "the People" or "the People of… the River, the Plains, the Wind, the Forest," etc. "The People" is the literal translation of Haida, Anishinaabe, Dene, Gwich'in, Inuit, Saan, and scores of other tribal names. Those stories, which anthropologists politely dismiss as mythology—and religious missionaries condemn as heresy—are taught to the children, while the anthropologist's story is either ignored or derided. History, indigenous peoples know, is almost always the self-generated mythology of an imperial power—settlers and missionaries regarded indigenous creation stories as, at worst, pagan heresy, and, at best, unscientific nonsense… as if *their* creation story, *their* genesis, were scientifically sound and made any sense.

Like many creation stories, the Haida's begins with Raven—the trickster, transformer, magician, healer, and creator of all things. There are long and short versions of the story. Here is how Haida master carver Bill Reid tells it:

> The great flood, which had covered the earth for so long, had at last receded and the sand of Rose Spit, Haida Gwaii, lay dry. Raven walked around the sand, eyes and ears alert for any unusual sight or sound to break the monotony. A flash of white caught his eye and there, right at his feet, half-buried in the sand, was a gigantic clamshell. He looked more closely and saw that the shell was full of little creatures cowering in terror in his enormous shadow. He leaned his great head close and, with his smooth trickster's tongue, coaxed and cajoled and coerced them to come out and play in his wonderful new shiny world. These little dwellers were the original Haida, the first humans.

There are more detailed accounts in Haida lore—one where Raven finds female humans in a giant vulva-shaped mollusk and coaxes them out to breed with the all-male clam humans—but those are the adult versions, less fit for young eyes and ears. So in school or by the fireside, it's the Bill Reid version that is told, accompanied by a photograph of his classic six-foot-tall cedar carving, which is permanently displayed in a circular room of its own in the Museum of Anthropology at the University of British Columbia in Vancouver, BC, which features one of the most impressive collections of Haida art in the world. (And Haida art is in almost every museum that features indigenous art.)

Anthropological accounts of the Haida's origins generally begin and end with sentences like "The Haida, a North American native culture, settled in the Canadian Queen Charlotte Islands and Alaska area over eight thousand years ago," indicating strong scientific uncertainty about where the first settlers of Haida Gwaii set out from, if from anywhere at all, and when they settled on Haida Gwaii. The alleged duration of settlement on the islands ranges up to seventeen thousand years, but the higher numbers are generally dismissed by ethnographers as "oral histories."

Tools, fish weirs, and other artifacts, some of the oldest archaeological finds in Canada, indicate that there was human settlement on the archipelago as far back as thirteen thousand years ago. Rarely is the Asia–Alaska (Bering) land bridge mentioned, although it's believed by many anthropologists to have been the original transit route for all North and South American native peoples, despite the fact that it ceased being open to transit fifteen to thirty-five thousand years ago, before the existence of any notable human civilizations. However, there is cultural and linguistic evidence that some tribes on both continents, the Haida among them, may have originated in Polynesia or Micronesia and found their way to American shores in ocean-worthy long boats similar in design to traditional Haida canoes. But when it comes to determining occupancy and defending sovereignty, does all that really matter?

After a few hundred generations in one place, it begins to matter less and less where a people wandered from, particularly as they develop a new language, a new religion, new art, ethics, music, their own laws, original metaphysics, and a whole new cosmology. So for all intents and purposes, it doesn't matter where the first Haida were born. They probably weren't "Haida" then anyway. They may have been nomads or explorers from a faraway place, another tribe with a different name. Haida culture, language, art, and laws were all created and evolved on the islands. So the trickster-Raven-and-clamshell story is as real and relevant as any other scenario. The Haida whose autonomy is today at issue certainly originated on Haida Gwaii. And that fact is central to the Haida's argument for sovereignty, and their claim for aboriginal title.

* * *

IT IS truly amazing that a few wanderers could wash up on a remote and climatically hostile archipelago and then essentially alone develop a complex, thriving civilization that eventually had its own written language and expressed itself to the world in art that Claude Lévi-Strauss considered as powerful and significant as anything produced in Europe. Most of Lévi-Strauss's colleagues in anthropology, too, place the Haida on their short lists of most exceptional cultures. "Every surviving tribe in the world seems to excel at something—hunting, fishing, foraging, cultivating honey, weaving, architecture, carving, singing, dancing, jewelry, tattooing, on and on," explained one anthropologist. "The Haida excel at just about everything." (For more on Haida architecture in particular, see sidebar on page 3.)

Explanations for Haida success, creativity, and cultural exceptionalism abound. The following are some key factors:

- Food security: Haida Gwaii and its surrounding water provide enough protein, vegetation, and fiber to feed fifteen thousand people without much cultivation, which it did at the height of the islands' population in the late nineteenth century. Yes, these people had to hunt, fish, and forage for food. But it was plentiful and accessible, so they never really had to worry about their food supply or spend a lot of time going after it. Unlike for so many aboriginal communities, famine was not a consideration. There isn't even a word for it in Haida. So there was time left for culture. Men carved, women wove, and Haida art flourished.

- Slaves: Like many warrior tribes and native communities that had to defend themselves from raiding parties, the Haida took slaves. Even as shocking as it seems today, taking slaves made humane and ethical sense at a time when the alternatives were either killing prisoners of war or sending them back to rejoin their armies and attack again. Most slaves were kept for seven to ten years before being released. By all indications, Haida slaves were well fed and well treated, some so well that many stayed after serving their time, married into the tribe, and became Haida… well, sort of Haida. Old-timers remember and occasionally kid their friends who have "slave blood." The Haida were one of the few people of color in the world to enslave white people, most of them prospectors, liquor traders, and others attempting to exploit the Haida or, worse, their women. Having slaves meant having time—more time for art. (For more on Haida slavery, see the sidebar on page 18.)

- Education: "The living generation accepts the responsibility to ensure that our heritage is passed on to following generations." So says the Constitution of the Haida Nation. Successful societies recognize that children are their future. And they do much better than ones who don't. And educated children promise a better future to any society. So the Haida have valued education—not residential school education forced upon them by the federal government, but public education close to home—with Haida teachers and a strong curricular emphasis on Haida culture and language and the idea of independence.

- Independence: This is a word you hear and read often on the islands, where it is now stated as an official goal of the Haida Nation. Of course, *independence* sets off loud alarms for sovereign states, even those that themselves once sought and won independence from an imperial power. But ask a Haida leader what they mean by *independence* and they will quickly assure you they don't seek secession or total autonomy. "We just do not want to be dependent on another power" is the way one Haida leader described their goal. "Independence is in our blood."

- Ferocity: No one messed with the Haida, ever. Warfare was swift, decisive, and regarded as a ceremonial act. Neighboring tribes attempting raids on the islands regretted their decisions. Uninvited gold miners and liquor traders were either enslaved or sent home with serious wounds. European explorers who even glanced at a Haida woman had their ships burned to the waterline. That ferocity is now transferred into a determination to be ruled and exploited by no one but themselves.

- Trading: Didn't matter what it was—otter pelts for kettles, seal skins for chisels, halibut for oolichan, gold for weapons, cedar for textiles, traps for firearms, or elk for goat—no one ever got the better of the Haida in a trade. Their uncompromising shrewdness survives to this day in every negotiation, transaction, meeting, and court appearance.

As this list attests, the Haida are clearly gifted in ways that few others civilizations are. But their main and most important gift is respect, which they regard as both a gift and a national possession. Not the respect they have earned worldwide for their remarkable art and tenacity, but the respect that they have for other things. *Yah'guudang*, they call it. It's the most revealing and important word in the Haida language. According to the Haida Land Use Vision of 2005, *Yah'guudang* "celebrates the ways our lives and spirits intertwine, and honors the responsibility we hold to future generations." Respect is the highest value in Haida culture, held intensely and openly by all Haida, young and old, for every thing and person worthy of respect—family, community, elders, and, yes, oneself. But central to it all and to Haida cosmology is "respect for all living things," the literal translation of *Yah'guudang*.

The Haida also exude respect for fellow humans, even when face-to-face with their adversaries or hostile media. But it is their deep respect for the spirit that they believe exists in everything, animate and inanimate, that makes them truly exceptional. Their respect shows. Haida matriarch April Churchill, a former vice president of the Haida Nation, warns the children, "When we are not respectful of the Creator's gifts, there are grave consequences. It's about knowing our place in the web of life, and how the fate of our culture runs parallel to the fate of the ocean, sky, and forest."[4]

The Haida are highly logical people who respect modern science (knowing that most of it is simply a textbook version of what they've known all along). "We agree with the Dalai Lama," April Churchill told me. "He says that if science disproved something he believed, he would go with the

Haida Slavery

THERE ARE dozens of conflicting accounts and descriptions of slavery on Haida Gwaii, including the ways slaves were taken, traded, bought, sold, and treated. Here, based on multiple common accounts, is what seems certain: the Haida had slaves.

4 From the Haida Land Use Vision (2005)

science."[5] And they are warriors who have never been conquered and refuse to be assimilated or colonized, although they are happy to live as equals with anyone of any origin who respects the biota of Haida Gwaii, which of course includes humans. About half the population of Haida Gwaii are non-Haida. They are citizens of Canada, not of Haida Gwaii, but they receive the respect of Haida citizens, who, like them, are also citizens of Canada and British Columbia, something they never asked for, but were granted anyway.[6]

* * *

THE NATIVE population of Haida Gwaii grew gradually over the centuries, reaching an estimated 15,000 by the mid-nineteenth

Truth is, many North and South American tribes enslaved one another, as did Africans.

At one point, up to 30 percent of the Haida population may have been slaves. Most Haida slaves were the defeated warriors of other First Nations that had the temerity to attack Haida Gwaii. With their prisoners of war, the Haida had three choices:

Kill them? Too harsh.

Send them home? To be rearmed and sent back for another assault? Dumb idea.

Enslave them humanely, for a probationary period, and then try to rehabilitate them before either releasing them or inviting them to stay on?

Option three appears to have won. So prisoners of war were definitely one source of slaves for the Haida. But there are

5 Churchill also explained to me why so many Haida were devout Christians. "Our cultural concept of love and respect is older than Christianity," she said, "and very close to Jesus's teachings. Like Christians, we see the Creator's work in all things."

6 The Haida word for white people is Yaatz-Haida. But Yaatz does not mean "white"; it means "iron." Whites who first visited Haida Gwaii were called "iron people" because they brought iron to the islands. And few things changed the culture, industry, and artistry of Haida Gwaii more than iron, which came in the form of axes, adzes, chisels, and awls that are still used by Haida builders, canoe makers, and pole carvers.

also accounts of Haida going on lightning raids to kidnap or capture slaves from neighboring tribes. And what seems certain is that the Haida are one of the few, if not the only, nonwhite civilizations in history to have enslaved white people. The whites were mostly British soldiers who either committed crimes while on leave, or worse, made eyes at a Haida woman—that could get your ship burned to the waterline with all sailors taken prisoner. But among the Haida's white slaves were also gold miners, thieves, and whiskey traders.

Haida slaves were a commodity, traded frequently for other commodities and occasionally used to pay debts and buy wives. A slave was allowed to marry, even to a Haida woman if she'd have him.

century, all living in 126 villages encircling the coastline. Then in 1860, smallpox found its way onto the islands, and by the end of the century, the Haida population was reduced to 588 people, all of whom had buried scores of relatives, some of them in shallow mass graves.[7] In the century that followed, the Haida increased their population by a factor of five, recovering about a third of their peak number.

Like so many other First Nation children in Canada and native people around the world, beginning in 1894, Haida youth were essentially abducted from their families by the federal government and sent away to "residential schools" to learn English and become Christian while

7 There are differing theories about how smallpox found its way onto Haida Gwaii. Some Haida believe it was "germ warfare"—a deliberate genocidal introduction of the virus with the sinister aim of annihilating an entire nation of people to grab their land and resources. Others believe it was brought back to the island by Haida who had visited Victoria during an outbreak of the disease there. Then there were those warm and beautiful Hudson's Bay blankets, traded for fish and furs, that infected people. Of course, this scenario begs the question as to whether or not the blankets were deliberately infected with the virus. Others say that whiskey traders and gold miners quite innocently carried the disease with them onto the islands. No one knows for sure. However, it caused a once proud and prosperous community to watch their population decline from fifteen thousand to six hundred souls in less than two generations.

unlearning their own language and cultural values. The aim of the federally contracted, church-run school systems was to "kill the Indian in the child," assimilate them into the colonial culture, and help them become cheap labor for private industry—serfs. The schools were also designed to sever First Nations peoples' ties to the land. But because there were so many remote villages and fish camps around the islands, it was fairly easy for Haida children to escape the round-up, and many did. As a result, much of Haida culture, personality, and self-determination survived the residential school era (for which Canada has recently apologized through the National Truth and Reconciliation Commission).

Although many Haida escaped the residential schools and were able to avoid assimilation, most have for one reason or another adopted European names. Some acquired a new name through marriage, but others just borrowed

But the children of slaves were enslaved. Slaves did menial work and paddled war canoes.

Where the legend gets dicey is in conflicting accounts of how the Haida treated their slaves. Rumors range from generous to brutal, from kindly to vicious. There's an oral history of a white slave remarking that he'd been well treated and never had a better meal than he'd had while enslaved by the Haida. But there are also possibly apocryphal tales of Haida sacrificing slaves as an offering to visiting dignitaries, and refusing to bury them on the islands when they died, instead simply throwing their corpses into the sea.

What most historians seem to agree with is that the Haida kept their slaves for a limited period, ranging from seven to ten years,

surnames from people they liked, respected, or admired. A few of their new names are anglicizations of Haida names. Edenshaw, a prominent surname on the islands, for example, derives from Iidansaa, which may have originally been a Tlingit name. No one seems to have forgotten their Haida names, though; in fact, some have made them exclusive, like Guujaaw, former president of the Haida Nation, whose anglo-name is Gary Edenshaw. Meanwhile, both his sons have kept the Edenshaw surname after attaching to it Haida first names Gwai and Jaalen. The current president is routinely and formally introduced as "Kil tlaats'gaa, President Peter Lantin." Some Haida names are so difficult to spell or pronounce, they are rarely used. Guujaaw's cousin Charlie Edenshaw's Haida name, for instance, is Daxiigang. Another Haida man, Abraham Jones, could go by Kilxhawgins if anyone outside his family and a few remaining Haida speakers could pronounce it. Place names are the same. The ancient villages of Hlghagilda, Qquuna, and Ghadaghaaxhiwaas are now known by the easier to pronounce and spell names Skidegate, Skedans, and Massett.

at which point they were either released or invited to stay in Haida Gwaii as second-class citizens. Some even married into the tribe, although until quite recently, the Haida seemed to remember who was and who was not descended from slavery, and for some reason, former slaves and their descendants all seemed to have settled in one community.

Haida society is matrilineal, not matriarchal. Although women are very powerful in Haida culture and politics, most hereditary chiefs and all but one president of the Haida Nation have been men (see sidebar about power, page 51). All families are divided into one of two moieties—Ravens or Eagles—following from their mother. Ravens can only marry Eagles and vice versa, an effective and still practiced built-in preventer of inbreeding.

While the almost five thousand First Nations of the world differ widely in many ways, they share the same essential problem, which is the assumptions carried across the seas by almost every European explorer: that discovery meant ownership, that whoever planted their flag on a shoreline first owned pretty much everything in sight, and that the discoverer was free to overtake and control anyone living there. This notion, which spread slowly across "discovered" continents, became an internationally recognized legal doctrine, cited for centuries, without authority or precedent, by lawyers and judges defending an imperial right to title and sovereignty.

The next six chapters set up the historical and legal context for any First Nation's struggle for self-determination and autonomy. If you're interested in only the Haida narrative, fast-forward to chapter 9.

3

The Problem

This people has no belief in God that amounts to anything.

Jacques Cartier

THE PROBLEM for the Haida, and indigenous peoples worldwide, was codified on May 4, 1493, when Pope Alexander VI, a corrupt libertine Borgia who ruled the Roman Catholic Church from 1492 to 1503, issued the papal bull Inter Caetera. Later renamed the Doctrine of Discovery, Alexander's papal bull granted the Spanish Crown all lands to the "west and south" of a pole-to-pole line "three hundred miles west and south of the Azores or the Cape Verde islands." Geographically, that really just covered a lot of salt water, because Vatican maps of the world were not accurate. What the pontiff really meant to say was "pretty much the rest of the known planet."

It remains unclear to the present whether Alexander was issuing a donation of land, a gift of sovereignty, or a feudal investiture (the transfer of a fief to a vassal). As things turned out, that really didn't matter, at least to the millions of people who lived west of Europe and would suffer for centuries under a doctrine that assumed, prima facie, that the Vatican and the Crowns of Europe controlled, if not owned, the world. Differing interpretations have been argued since the bull was issued, with some saying that it was only meant to transform the occupation of land into lawful sovereignty. Others, including the Spanish Crown and their conquistadors, interpreted it in the widest possible sense, assuming that it gave Spain full title on any lands discovered and Spanish hegemony over non-Christian peoples encountered anywhere in the world by Christian Spanish explorers.[8]

What is important and relevant is that forms, passages, and interpretations of the bull have for centuries since been cited and used repeatedly as binding legal doctrine by parliaments and courts the world over to interpret discovery as possession, and justify the assumption of European sovereignty over non-Christian communities on every continent.

The bull is written to "Our very dear son in Christ, Ferdinand, King, and our very dear daughter in Christ, Isabella, Queen of Castile, León, Aragon, Sicily, and Granada." It expresses the deepest hope "that in our times the Catholic faith and the Christian religion will be exalted… the health of souls be cared for, and barbarous nations overthrown and brought to the faith."

---

8 Portuguese explorers cited the similarly worded *Romanus Pontifex*, written in 1454 by Pope Nicholas V to King Afonso V of Portugal, confirming his dominion over the Canary Islands and all land in Africa south of Cape Bojador (most of the continent). "The Roman pontiff, successor of the key-bearer of the heavenly kingdom and vicar of Jesus Christ," the pope began, "contemplating with a father's mind all the several climes of the world and the characteristics of all the nations dwelling in them and seeking and desiring the salvation of all…" and went on to grant Portugal title to all lands found and sovereignty over all their heathen occupants.

The purpose of this huge gift of land, almost half the planet, was to have "the name of our Savior carried into those regions, to lead the peoples dwelling in those islands and countries to embrace the Christian religion… with the stout hope and trust… that Almighty God will further your undertakings."

The pontiff then deputized the king and his heirs "with full and free power, authority, and jurisdiction of every kind" over everyone living in the new lands, and he instructed them to "appoint to the aforesaid mainlands and islands worthy, God-fearing, learned, skilled, and experienced men, in order to instruct the aforesaid inhabitants and residents in the Catholic faith and train them in good morals."

He continues, "Furthermore, under penalty of excommunication to be incurred ipso facto should anyone thus contravene, I strictly forbid all persons of whatsoever rank, even imperial and royal, or of whatsoever estate, degree, order, or condition, to dare without your special permit or that of your aforesaid heirs and successors, to go for the purpose of trade or any other reason to the islands or mainlands." In other words, all wealth found there was to be reserved for the king and queen, none of it for the conquistadors or other explorers.

And the only man on earth with a direct line to God closed with this wish: "We trust in Him from whom empires and governments and all good things proceed, that, should you, with the Lord's guidance, pursue this holy and praiseworthy undertaking, in a short while your hardships and endeavors will attain the most felicitous result, to the happiness and glory of all Christendom."

The Doctrine of Discovery, also known as the Discovery Doctrine, became a canon of international law cited by courts and governments for centuries, although many who have used the term have had no idea of its origins. To one degree or another, its basic sentiment became justification for the occupation and subjugation of First Nations on every continent, and central to the message of Euro-imperialism: You are primitive heathens who have no idea how to manage yourselves or your land. And we do, so we'll take over and do it for you. If you resist our kindness, or our sovereignty, or Jesus, or worse, claim title to your land, we'll move you onto reservations. Resist that and we'll simply have to annihilate you.

Writing for the entire US Supreme Court in *Johnson v. M'Intosh*, in 1823 Justice John Marshall cited what he understood to be the Discovery Doctrine to argue that ownership of land comes into existence by virtue of discovery of that land, a rule that had been observed by all European countries with settlements in the New World. "The history of America, from its discovery to the present day, proves, we think, the universal recognition of these principles," Marshall wrote. Over the years, Canadian lawyers litigating aboriginal land claims have frequently cited both Marshall and the Doctrine of Discovery.

The doctrine has been cited in other Native American litigation. In *Cherokee Nation v. Georgia*, it was used to support the concept that tribal lands were not independent states but "domestic dependent nations." And *Oliphant v. Suquamish Indian Tribe* and *Duro v. Reina* both used the doctrine to prohibit tribes from criminally prosecuting non-Indians or Indians who were not a member of the prosecuting tribe.

The doctrine was cited by the US Supreme Court as recently as 2005, in *City of Sherrill, NY v. Oneida Nation*, which in part read, "Under the Doctrine of Discovery, fee title (ownership) to the lands occupied by Indians when the colonists arrived became vested in the sovereign—first the discovering European nation and later the original states and the United States."

Canada, which is a hundred years younger than the United States, and which eventually laid claim to Haida Gwaii, closely followed American jurisprudence and case law affecting Native Americans, citing many of the aforementioned cases in its own litigation against First Nation claims for title and sovereignty, including litigation against the Haida.

In retrospect, the hubris and hypocrisy of European powers during the entire colonial era was astounding. Spain, for example, Europe's spearhead into the New World, felt quite justified in expelling the Moors, who had invaded and occupied their homeland, in what they called El Reconquista, but felt completely comfortable themselves conquering and occupying the homelands of millions in the New World, reading aloud in Spanish as they landed a *Requerimiento* (a "Charter of Conquest") demanding that their hosts, who had never heard a word of Spanish or the name of Jesus, immediately adopt the Christian faith and accept the king and queen of Spain as their rulers. And the slightest hesitation on the part of natives to comply led to some of the most brutal atrocities in human history.[9] The French and British weren't as brutal as the Spanish, but their hubris and conceit was equal to anyone's.

Rather than following a marching order from a monarch in Madrid or Lisbon, British and French settlers were more likely to be following God's command to have dominion over nature and conquer the wilderness. The only problem with that order

9 Some Spaniards took exception to this approach. Father Bartolome de Las Casas, for example, condemned his countrymen's treatment of North American Indians as "unjust and tyrannical."

was there were people in the way. Yes, they were human, but they were "morally and intellectually deformed" humans—"noble savages,"[10] but savages nonetheless.

* * *

THE FIRST European monarch to reconsider the Doctrine of Discovery was Britain's George III, the king America learned to despise. The earliest violent conflict faced by early British settlers in North America was with French colonists rather than with Indians, although in the seven years of war with France, which was fought in Europe and America and on the ocean between them, the Indians generally sided with the French, who as colonialists had been more just and accommodating with them than the British.

The Treaty of Paris, which marked the end of the war, granted Britain a great deal of valuable North American land. But the new land also gave rise to some serious problems, not the least of which were the Indians who had fought with the French and feared the British Crown would assume sovereignty and claim title over their nations. Ottawa chief Pontiac in particular led numerous attacks against British colonial settlements. Partly to defuse Indian concerns, King George III issued the Royal Proclamation of 1763, which recognized aboriginal governments as original landowners.

10 In English, the phrase *noble savage* first appeared in poet Dryden's heroic play, *The Conquest of Granada* (1672):

"I am as free as nature first made man,
Ere the base laws of servitude began,
When wild in woods the noble savage ran."

However, Dryden may have learned the phrase from a 1609 travelogue about Canada by the French explorer Marc Lescarbot, in which there was a chapter with the heading "The Savages are Truly Noble." Anthropologists of every nationality eventually adopted the phrase and used it frequently in their writing.

The origins of "morally and intellectually deformed" are less certain. The phrase is found often in the journals and letters of early priests and missionary settlers of the New World.

The main intent of the Proclamation was to limit western expansion of the American colonies into Pontiac's realm beyond the Appalachian Mountains. Land beyond the mountains, the eastern watershed of the Mississippi River, was declared "the Indian Reserve," and the Proclamation led to the negotiation of over four hundred treaties with First Nations in the United States and Canada. But its real aim was to divert British settlers north to Nova Scotia and south to Florida. The Proclamation was extremely unpopular with land speculators in Britain and expansionist settlers like Daniel Boone, who continued to lead his followers west beyond the Appalachians. Historians still debate its effect on the American Revolution, but the Proclamation was certainly an aggravation mentioned frequently by pamphleteers of the time.

The line drawn by the Proclamation was never intended to be a permanent border between white and aboriginal lands, but rather a temporary, shiftable boundary that could be extended farther west in an orderly, "lawful" manner as settlers moved into the heartland. The Proclamation outlawed the private purchase of Native American land, an action which had created problems in the past for both sellers and buyers. Instead, all future land purchases were to be made by the Crown. Colonials were forbidden to move beyond the line and settle on native lands, and officials were forbidden to grant ground or lands without royal approval. In this way, the Proclamation gave the Crown a monopoly on all future land purchases from American Indians.

Prominent American colonials who regarded western lands as a war prize were embittered, particularly those in settlements that already existed beyond the Proclamation line. Colonial blood had been shed to defeat and expel the French and Indians, not to cede land to them. What was to be said for American colonists who had already settled the Ohio Valley? They joined forces with land speculators in Britain to lobby the government to move the line farther west. Their efforts were successful, and the boundary line was adjusted in a series of treaties with the Native Americans that opened much of what is now Kentucky and West Virginia to British settlement.

The Proclamation continued to govern the status of indigenous land in British North America, especially Upper Canada and Rupert's Land (the vast area surrounding Hudson's Bay), where it still forms the basis of land claims of Canadian First Nations, Inuit, and Métis. Historians disagree on whether the Proclamation recognized or undermined tribal sovereignty, but it certainly did establish the important precedent that indigenous populations had certain rights to the lands they occupied. This precedent would become vital to Haida interests in years to come.

Some scholars and aboriginal lawyers still regard the Proclamation as a fundamental document for First Nations land claims and self-government, as it was "the first legal recognition by the British Crown of Aboriginal rights"[11] and imposed a fiduciary duty of care on the Crown. On the other hand, the intent of and promises made in the Proclamation have also been argued to be of a temporary nature, only meant to appease the native peoples, who were becoming increasingly resentful of settler encroachments on their lands and were capable of becoming a serious threat to British colonial settlement.

Some believe that the British were simply trying to convince First Nations people that there was nothing to fear from the

11 Douglas R. Francis, Richard Jones, and Donald B. Smith, *Origins: Canadian History to Confederation* 6th ed. (Toronto: Nelson Education Ltd., 2009), 157.

colonists. Others argue that the Proclamation affirms aboriginal powers of self-determination. And there remain First Nations that still embrace that interpretation. In October 2013, the 250th anniversary of the Royal Proclamation was celebrated in Ottawa with a meeting of Indian leaders and the governor general of Canada. Meanwhile, the aboriginal movement Idle No More held birthday parties for the monumental document at various locations across Canada.

Of course, celebrating the Royal Proclamation is something of a hollow gesture as most colonists and colonial governments at every level have ignored its best intentions and run things for two or more centuries as if George III had been insane, which, of course, he was. As it turned out, most of the four hundred treaties mandated by the Proclamation were eventually broken, and millions of acres of land were stolen "fair and square" from one First Nation after another. The Haida would be among the last First Nations in the Americas to suffer that fate, as all these proclamations, doctrines, and treaties set in motion the structures and ethical frameworks that would define their struggle. They were also among the first to fight back.

Thanks to revisionist historians like Charles Mann, Jared Diamond, and others, the true state of the non-European world before the sixteenth century is gradually becoming clear to us. It was certainly a very different place than European explorers thought they would find, and a somewhat different place than they told their patrons they had found.

Of course, their patrons' interests were primarily in gold…

And, well… souls.

4

Gold and Souls

These savages will give us trouble yet.

Francis Campble

"SAVE SOME souls for the pope if you can, but bring home gold" was the common marching order given to Vasco Núñez de Balboa, John Cabot, Juan Ponce de León, Henry Hudson, Jacques Cartier, Hernando Cortés, Samuel de Champlain, Vasco de Gama, Ferdinand Magellan, Sir Francis Drake, Francisco Pizarro, Amerigo Vespucci, and scores of lesser-known explorers and adventurers sent across the oceans to find and take booty for their patrons. Souls were the excuse, the high-minded mission designed to please the Holy Mother Church, but the ultimate quarry was gold, spices, some timber for ship building, furs for aristocrats, and, ultimately, some productive land.

By 1550, most of these bold men had made landfall somewhere far from Europe and discovered that there were people living, even thriving, where they were least expected. In fact, there were well in excess of five thousand nations scattered about five other continents on the planet, some of them among the most advanced, civilized, and sophisticated societies that have ever appeared anywhere—the Incas, Persians, Chinese, Aztecs, Japanese, Mayans, Egyptians, and Mesopotamians.

They were big, complex, scientifically astute civilizations with sophisticated populations in the millions that created huge well-designed and brilliantly engineered cities set in vast expanses of cultivated land connected by roads, aqueducts, irrigation canals, and sewage systems. Some were long gone by the time Europeans found them, buried with the fabulous art and artifacts that attested to the wealth and ingenuity of peoples that matched the power and creativity of the Greeks, Romans, Spaniards, Portuguese, Scandinavians, or Brits at the peak of their splendors. But some were still standing, prime targets for conquest, and conquered they were. But most of the nations out there in the unexplored, undiscovered world of the Middle Ages were tiny, remote, and by European standards quite primitive. When they disappeared, their infrastructures decayed into the jungle in less than a generation, their nonmetallic utensils and art along with them. They left no history, sparse architecture, no written language, and no lasting or valued artifacts beyond a few arrowheads or cave wall sketches of antelopes and bison. So it was easy to dismiss them as simple savages, worthy of a line or two in an explorer's log, but unworthy of so much as a footnote in the heroic history of mankind.

But even the most primitive societies, we are now learning through more precise archaeology and anthropology, were as human as any other, with cultures, values, unique social systems, hierarchies, ethics, mathematics, moieties, agriculture, cosmologies, architecture, civil engineering, religions, and in some cases truly remarkable art forms. In their logs, explorers occasionally made note of the exceptional talents and decencies of the aboriginals they encountered:

> "They are really better to us than we are to them" (John Lawson, 1709).

> "They will seldom injure a Christian, except if given cause for it" (Christoph von Graffenried, 1711).

> "They strive after a sincere honesty, hold strictly to their promises, cheat and injure no one. They willingly give shelter to others and are both useful and loyal to their guests" (Francis Daniel Pastorius, 1712).

> "We all know that very bright talents may be lodged under a very dark skin" (William Byrd, 1728).

> "They keep their word, and hate lies" (Philip Georg Friedrich von Reck, 1736).

But a lot of post-contact social commentary was racist and dismissive:

> "They are a warlike race, and extremely cruel" (Amerigo Vespucci, 1502).

> "This people has no belief in God that amounts to anything" (Jacques Cartier, 1535).

> "Among themselves they are almost always engaged in war" (Rev. Johann Martin Bolzius, 1750).

> "These savages will give us trouble yet" (Francis Campble, 1740).

Because the Eurocentric Judeo-Christian worldview was so different from most aboriginal worldviews, the conflict that arose between European explorers and the peoples they discovered was essentially one of misunderstanding. The problem was, and still is, that "cultural misunderstanding" became an excuse and a polite term for racism, unjustified ethnic superiority, and a persistent religious conceit that says "Only *we* have found the one true God." That conviction alone has led to more human bloodshed, more oppression, more injustice, and more usurpation of sovereignty than any other disagreement in the five-hundred-year conflict between First Nations and nations that believed *they* were the first nations, or that the nations they found outside Europe weren't really nations at all. People who came to be called "First Nations" were, to their discoverers, insignificant communities of people, people of color, "a subhuman species" that had found a hunting ground, built some lean-tos, tipis, or hogans and a longhouse next to it, and needed to be conquered, subjugated, and baptized before they could become part of the human community—part of a true nation, the imperial Christian

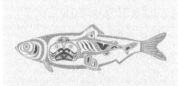

Maps Are Power

As much as guns and warships, maps have been the weapons of imperialism.

J. Brian Harley,
historian

MAPS HAVE been weapons of imperialism, it is true, but they have also been used effectively to reclaim and defend millions of square miles of indigenous territory. Whether for good or evil, maps are

nation manifestly destined to embrace them.

Very few, if any, of the indigenous communities outside Europe actually believed that about themselves, although some of their leaders pretended to, simply to avoid the inevitable genocide they had reason to believe awaited them if they refused to submit to "the covenant, the sword and the word of the Lord."

As the colonization of the planet progressed, the imperial interest in gold gradually expanded to include just about every imaginable source of wealth—timber, metal, oil, gas, coal, medicines, gems, food crops, germplasms, fresh water, and, of course, arable land. Standing in the way of most of those resources have been native people, who for the most part harbor a very different view of land, property, wealth, ecology, and economics than European colonizers. It's been the making of a gigantic culture clash, an intractable conflict of interests, and

powerful weapons. And few have been more aware of this than the Haida, who with the Gowgaia Institute used mapping as the first step in developing a comprehensive Land Use Vision for the islands (nicknamed Haida LUV). Together, they mapped protected areas and sacred places honored by their ancestors, including the locations of abandoned villages, burial grounds, monumental cedars, culturally modified trees, and seasonal fish camps. The process led to the signing, seven years later in December 2007, of a protocol with British Columbia that laid out a long-term strategic land-use plan for the islands based on ecosystem-based management. The Council of the Haida Nation also announced plans to purchase TFL 39, a valuable

a worldwide abuse of consent that's lasted five hundred years and persists to this day. Souls are still of interest to evangelicals, but the quest for mammon has overwhelmed and surpassed them, particularly the quest for land, and, more recently, water. Most of the unexploited resources remaining today sit on or under indigenous lands.

As land became the preferred quarry of New World settlers, the dynamic between First and Second Nations shifted. Aboriginals were not particularly possessive about gold, and millions of them were quite willing to release their souls to Jesus, whose teachings and ethics were not unlike a lot of their own. And most indigenous communities around the world were quite willing to trade renewable resources like fur, spices, silver, and salt for metal tools and guns. But land was another matter. Land was life, and it was sacred. Most of the serious conflicts, treaties, lawsuits, and reconciliations between native peoples and European settlers have been over land, its title, and its uses. Unlike fur and spices, land was simply not for trading.

It has always been rather difficult for the Euro-colonial mind to understand native peoples' relationship to land, or grasp the

tree farm license covering one-quarter of the islands, with $38 million from the Gwaii Trust created at the formation of Gwaii Haanas.

Protected areas under ecosystem-based management now comprise 52 percent of the entire archipelago, and the annual cut of timber on the islands has been reduced from 1.7 million cubic meters a year to 800,000, all of it now under Haida tenure. This could not have been accomplished without maps.

difference between living *on* and living *with* the land. That tiny one-word difference has been the hardest thing for the Haida to get across, in all their struggles, communications, and litigations with government and extractive industry.

For the Haida, living *with* the land is not only right living, it is the only way to survive. Living *on* the land is seeing it as a platform, a substrate upon which life and economics proceed, without much concern about what's underfoot. Living with the land is the aboriginal way. And individual ownership of it is, to most aboriginal communities of the world, a mistake. In the Haida worldview, land does not belong to people; people belong to the land.

Before a First Nation can gain or regain title or sovereignty, its people should probably first understand how they lost it, how it was "extinguished." So history is vital. And the Haida know their history—not only their own, but also the history of the colonial powers that "discovered" their land and without hesitation claimed title to it. And they know that the imperial claim of title was based on a capricious letter written over five hundred years ago by a corrupt Italian libertine posing as God's emissary to the entire planet.

After Haida Gwaii had thrived as a nation for ten to twelve thousand years, it became part of Canada. It could as easily have become part of Russia, the USA, or Spain, as at one point or another during the colonial period, explorers from all those nations discovered the archipelago and traded with the Haida. But faced with an independent tribe of ferocious warriors who had never been conquered or defeated and were known to enslave their attackers, even white attackers, no one really wanted to conquer the Haida or claim their islands until 1871, when British Columbia joined the Canadian Confederation. Since the islands were only ninety miles offshore, and since it had the British Navy at its back, BC planted the Union Jack on Haida shores and claimed the place as its own, an extension of a larger colony of which it had recently become a province. Overnight, Haida Gwaii became a vassal state, BC its satrap.

Then known to the colonizers as the Queen Charlotte Islands, Haida Gwaii became one of 198 First Nations overtaken by the new province. Although aboriginals far outnumbered European settlers, none of them had a say or a vote as to whether or not to join the Confederation. The Haida have been fighting back ever since, for self-determination, sovereignty, aboriginal title, and something they define in their own terms as "independence." And in doing so, they've inadvertently developed a series of tactics that form the ingredients of an ideal playbook for indigenous strategy that should be useful just about anywhere in the world.

But before they could develop their own strategy for sovereignty and title, they set out to understand the meaning and history of the terms, beginning with sovereignty.

5

Sovereignty

*And it will be seen that there exists perhaps
no conception the meaning of which is more
controversial than that of sovereignty.*

Lassa Oppenheim

IT IS often said that all arguments, all disputes, are in the end semantic. So what are the semantics of sovereignty? Are they clear and concise, or, as is so often the case, are they tortured, murky, and pliable?

Sovereignty is indeed one of the slipperiest terms in our political lexicon. Few others have changed in meaning, significance, and consequence as frequently over the past five hundred years. And each change in the definition of sovereignty, some of them explosively sudden, has brought new forms and intensities of governance to (or in opposition to) millions of people. The main reasons for this are the relative youth of the term, the shifting loci of political power, and the coevolving natures of human behavior, politics, language, and human rights. The only thing certain about sovereignty is that it's something everyone seems to want, and none more so than people who don't have it because it was taken from them by people who either claim or believe they never had it to begin with.

Vaguely defined by consensus, *sovereignty* is today regarded as legitimate authority exercised inside a bordered area recognized as a state or nation. A sovereign claims supreme authority at home and independent authority overseas. A country's sovereignty demands respect by mere virtue of its recognition as a nation-state, with a name, borders, a capital city, a flag… and, with a few exceptions, an army.[12] The idea of sovereignty being owned or exercised by a people or a single ethnicity disappeared with the formation of America and other melting-pot nations around the world.

The modern concept of state sovereignty surfaced during two centuries (the sixteenth and seventeenth) of religious and political warfare in Europe. When the word first came into common use, sovereignty still flowed directly from God, through the Vatican. It was gradually bestowed by the pope to what the Holy Roman Empire dubbed *regna*—mini-empires, most of them feudal, under monarchs who were granted political legitimacy through "the divine right of kings."

Kings and queens were *legibus solutus*—free from the bonds of law, subordinate to no one but the pope, and constitutionally independent. As sovereigns they reigned supreme; they were as much religious figures as the pope himself was a political figure. Such was the state of Christendom. Furthermore, anointed

---

12 The exceptions are Costa Rica, Dominica, Grenada, Kiribati, Liechtenstein, the Marshall Islands, Micronesia, Palau, Samoa, the Solomon Islands, Tuvalu, and Vatican City, all of which have police or gendarmeries, but not armed forces capable of staging war on other nations.

monarchs commanded forces that assured compliance with their every order and mission, particularly the mission of dispatching well-armed Christian explorers to subdue and convert "pagan savages" in the New World.

As time wore on and wars over territory and revolutions for power tore Europe asunder, new nations were created on the continent. Sovereignty was gradually redistributed from monarchs to an illusive new political entity called "the state." And as human members of states assumed the right to rule themselves, the notion of self-determination emerged, although it wasn't given that name until years after it was asserted by people who through culture, language, and occupation bestowed on their communities and homelands a definition of *self* around which they assumed the right to draw boundaries and determine their place, and their citizens, a "nation-state." The operative ideas here, and for the Haida particularly, are the words *place* and *people*, and how they are defined—for those definitions, coupled with a distinct, bordered geographical territory, are the sine qua non of self-determination, and ultimately of sovereignty and independence. The Haida argument for sovereignty is based principally on the legal semantics of *people* and *place*,

Haida Power

SURFACE POWER in Haida Gwaii—the power that governments have to deal with, the power that media covers and lawyers interpret, the power that protects Haida sovereignty and independence—resides in the Council of the

Haida Nation (the islands' federal government). But true power in the Haida Nation is covert. It derives from deep guidance transmitted by spiritual ancestors through small, select committees of living elder women, "women of high esteem," also described to me by one of them, April Churchill, as "women past their moon."

Before a chief or other patriarch makes an important decision or steps out of the community to broker power, he spends time with his five- or six-member committee of elder women, who counsel him on how to deal with external powers. April describes the Haida way of power:

The man will step forward to speak for the clan, but behind that

which, cobbled together, created their concept of *nation*.

Unbeknownst to Europeans struggling through wars for sovereignty and self-determination, lasting anywhere from a month to a century, thousands of settlers elsewhere around the world had for centuries been expanding and converting their hunting grounds into small self-governed nations like Haida Gwaii, some of which merged with other tribal nations to form powerful and well-armed political forces like the Iroquois Confederacy and Tecumseh's pan-Indian alliance. And although history rarely recorded them, there were wars over boundaries and hunting grounds on every continent—small but often ferocious border wars and skirmishes for self-determination, like the vicious mid-seventeenth-century Beaver Wars between the Wendat and the Haudenosaunee (aka the Huron and Iroquois). Eventually, peace was made, borders agreed upon, and separate and equal First Nations created.

Once a First Nation like the Huron or Iroquois Confederacy was formed and borders determined, sovereignty within them was simply assumed. Although there was and still is no word for sovereignty in most indigenous languages, the notion of its being imposed by a pope or European imperial power that believed sheer force justified their control was repugnant to indigenous communities around the world. Some embraced the faith, but few embraced the conqueror. Once native peoples learned about sovereignty, however, they got the idea to assert it for themselves. "Colonialism provoked anti-colonialism" is the way Canadian-born political scientist Robert Jackson describes the process.[13]

* * *

13 Jackson, *Sovereignty* (Cambridge: Polity Press, 2007).

man is a group of women, who have a knowledge and strength that men weren't born with. It is the women of high esteem who sit behind the men and give them advice. And it is the wise men, our chiefs, who take the counsel of women who are the fiber and the strength behind them. Our women are powerful because they are the ones who for centuries have been enforcing stewardship and sustainability. We are caretakers of the land and progenitors of the nation.

This method of power transmission may seem excessively spiritual, even a little "woo-woo," to the modern western mind. But it has some material support. A central purpose of all indigenous oral traditions is to keep wisdom alive. In most aboriginal languages, there is a word for the people who store and transmit the wisdom of ancestors that was given to them orally by their elders. "Wisdom Keepers" are selected by their community because the people who interact with them every day regard them as wise enough to recognize ancestral advice that still makes sense, still works. They can pass that wisdom on as guidance and toss anything that turned out to be bad judgment into the dustbin of history. The selection of Wisdom Keepers differs from community to community. The women-past-their-moon model is not uniquely Haida, but it's rare.

The system seems to work in Haida Gwaii because Haida men in

FOR ABORIGINALS, sovereignty has never been something to be won, or lost and won back, or surrendered by way of conquest. It's been something they had always possessed and never relinquished. It was a gift from the creator, a basic national right to be preserved, and if usurped, to be recovered from "the iron people," with their long swords and muskets, who assumed that stealing sovereignty was justified by superior force or some outrageous declaration like Pope Alexander's Doctrine of Discovery.

US Supreme Court Chief Justice John Marshall, in *Johnson v. M'Intosh* and other rulings, clearly bought into the idea that the ambitions of the conqueror trumped the rights of the conquered. Writing for a unanimous court in *Johnson*, he observed that Christian European nations had assumed "ultimate dominion" over American lands during the "Age of Discovery." Upon discovery, Marshall wrote, Indians lost "their rights to complete sovereignty, as independent nations," retaining a mere right of "occupancy" of their lands, an aboriginal form of title that could be extinguished. And, of course, title *was* extinguished, by conquest, and Indian tribes were designated "domestic dependent nations" incorporated into the United States, the government of which bore the inherent right to extinguish both title and sovereignty.

In other words, the First Nations in America were now subject to the ultimate authority of Latin Christendom to claim possession of their land and their sovereignty. The colonizers had bravely crossed the treacherous Atlantic to take full possession of two gigantic continents, simply by planting a flag on the shoreline. The sovereignty of the Crowns of Spain, Portugal, France, Holland, and Britain was assumed over all land west of that shoreline, on the strength of a papal bull. Whatever aboriginal rights existed did so at the pleasure of those Crowns and could be extinguished at any time.

While sovereignty became something that could be lost in a heartbeat, it has never been something that could be won back power truly believe that it is only through elder women—women whom they have known all their lives, women past their moon, derided in most cultures as crones or "women past their prime"—that wisdom that truly works can be objectively selected and accurately transmitted.

What I describe in the rest of this book attests to the strong possibility that Haida men are right about that. Something is certainly working for the Haida, whose methods and expression of power in Canada and British Columbia are paying big dividends for them.

without a struggle. That happens gradually, step by step, court case by court case, petition by petition, treaty by treaty. And it is happening. First Nations around the world have adopted an impressive array of strategies for recovering and preserving their sovereignty. As water eventually erodes rock, indigenous cultures and their values are slowly dissolving the sovereignties forced upon them by imperialists.[14]

***

AS THE term implies, self-determination bestows a right upon any community to determine itself, where to determine also means "to govern." Thus, self-determination and sovereignty have become inseparably linked as cardinal rights sought by First Nations imploring colonial states to at the very least accept "divisible," "parallel," or "shared" sovereignty, similar in form to the terms the once completely sovereign nations of the European Union agreed to, or the constitutional relationship between federal and state or provincial governments in national federations like the United States and Canada, or the less formal power arrangements between counties and incorporated municipalities within them.

As sovereignty has evolved in the world, as a word and a political reality, it is now almost everywhere shared by two or more political subdivisions within the same borders. The few exceptions are totalitarian national governments, monarchies, and dictatorships, where sovereignty flows from a single source. And of course

---

14 It would not be until late in the twentieth century that progressive Catholics would petition Pope John Paul II to formally revoke the Vatican's Doctrine of Discovery and recognize the human rights of "non-Christian" indigenous peoples. In 1992 in Santo Domingo, on the five-hundredth anniversary of Christopher Columbus landing there, John Paul confessed and begged forgiveness for the sins of his church in the Spanish conquest of America. He repeated a similar confession in 2000 when, kneeling at the Holy Doors of the Great Jubilee, he begged forgiveness for Catholics who had violated "the rights of ethnic groups and peoples, and sowed contempt for their cultures and religious traditions."

indigenous First Nations, having mostly been denied sovereignty altogether.[15] Nevertheless, as a consequence of globalization and the international struggle for human rights, the arc of political power, and justice, is bending gradually toward shared models of sovereignty.

Self-determination, incidentally, does not mean receiving citizenship or the right to vote in someone else's colony, both of which are generally regarded by most indigenous peoples as mere extensions of assimilation, to some even a violation of sovereignty. The Iroquois, for instance, regarded legislation that granted their people national citizenship in the US or Canada as "an extension of colonial occupation."[16]

To many modern states, *self-determination* is a threatening term, associated as it so often is with companion sentiments like independence, decolonization, or even worse, secession. It is the fear of those outcomes that has driven more than seventy imperial nations around the globe to vigorously, at times violently, oppose native self-determination and First Nation sovereignty.

Contemporary debates on the principle of self-determination focus on two questions: Who are the peoples entitled to this self-definition, to this legal right? And how far does the right extend? Domestic and international bodies have defined the term *peoples* to include subnational groups that are part of a larger

15 The United Nations is not sovereign. The European Union is sort of sovereign (its sovereignty is limited). The federal government of the United States of America is more sovereign, but not completely. Its sovereignty is shared with the states, as is Canada's with its provinces, and theirs in turn with municipalities… and more recently with a gradually increasing number of First Nations such as Haida Gwaii.

16 Here is how Clinton Rickard, chief of the Tuscarora, described the Iroquois objection to the US Indian Citizen Act of 1924: "To us it seemed like the United States government was just trying to get rid of its treaty obligations and make us into taxpaying citizens who could sell their homelands and end up in city slums… The Citizenship Act did pass despite our strong opposition. By its provisions all Indians were automatically made citizens whether they wanted to be so or not. This was a violation of our sovereignty. Our citizenship was in our own nations. We had a great attachment to our style of government. We wished to remain treaty Indians and preserve our ancient rights. There was no great rush among my people to go out and vote in white man's elections. Anyone who did so was denied the privilege of becoming a chief or clan mother in our nation."

territorial sovereign unit. When one considers the common factors that make up these subnational groups—such as common racial, ethnic, linguistic, religious, or cultural history; some claim to territory or land; and a shared sense of political, economic, social, and cultural goals—indigenous peoples easily meet the criteria.

But sovereignty has never been permanent, in its application or its meaning. It could disappear altogether as a concept. Or it could evolve into new forms of authority practiced independently by thousands of small nations that exist on the planet. Indeed, the evolving and ever-shifting definition and redefinition of *sovereignty* is the very thing that has allowed indigenous nations to take the issue to courts around the world and win back some of the rights and autonomy lost through colonization, or at the very least establish dual or shared sovereignty with their host nations. It is in this regard that the Haida are leading the way.

It's called "native title" in Australia, "original Indian title" in the US, and "customary title" in New Zealand. International lawyers are more likely to call it "indigenous title" and regard it as a common law doctrine shared by many nation-states that support the right of indigenous peoples within those states to customary land tenure after the assumption of sovereignty by the colonial power.

Most indigenous peoples, including the Haida, have their own preferred name for all those forms of land tenure— "aboriginal title."

6

Title Wave

We don't actually claim the land. It's the government who claims our land.

Guujaaw[17]

TO MOST international lawyers, land title is a concept of jurisdictional and economic definition, jurisdictional being the power to make decisions about human conduct, economic being the right to use land for the sustenance of the people who live on it. Aboriginal title in most nations that recognize it confers a degree of jurisdiction, although the extent is rarely made clear. What is clear is that aboriginal title derives from prior occupation and use, not from ownership.

The advent of aboriginal title represents one of the most remarkable, complex, and controversial legal developments of the late twentieth century. Overnight, it has changed the legal status

17 Former president of the Haida Nation.

of indigenous peoples throughout the world. It has given sudden substance to tribal claims of title over traditional lands, moving them up the national agenda and jolting them out of a previous culture of government inattention.

In a series of landmark cases around the world, national courts have adopted an argument for aboriginal title developed by a handful of influential scholars, first in western Canada, then in New Zealand, and finally in Australia. By the beginning of the millennium, the doctrine had spread to Malaysia, Belize, and southern Africa and has since had a profound impact upon the rapid development of international law regarding indigenous rights.

Requirements of proof for recognition of aboriginal title, the content of the title, the methods of extinguishing it, and the availability of compensation vary from country to country. But nearly all jurisdictions agree that aboriginal title is inalienable—it cannot be given or taken away. In most jurisdictions, it cannot be sold, except to the national government (only Malaysia allows aboriginal title to be sold between indigenous peoples). And almost everywhere, it is held collectively. But perhaps most important of all is the fact that the land in question is invariably regarded as sacred by the people who had been its stewards before it was appropriated, something that has been either disrespected or ignored by imperial powers who tend to regard land as a lifeless commodity containing extractable resources.

* * *

ABORIGINAL TITLE was first acknowledged by the British government in the early nineteenth century, but not in response to litigation. It was merely an interpretation of the thirty-year-old Royal Proclamation of 1763. The kind of significant title litigation that resulted in court victories for indigenous peoples did not occur until recent decades. The majority of those cases have been litigated in the former British colonies of Australia, Canada, Malaysia, New Zealand, and the United States. Aboriginal title has since become an important area of comparative law, with many cases now cited as persuasive authority across jurisdictions. Most international attorneys today believe that the doctrine is applicable in all common-law legal systems. At least, they try their title cases with that assumption.

Aboriginal title is often connected to indigenous rights, either influencing or being influenced by non-title issues, such as whether the government owes a fiduciary duty to indigenous peoples. While the assumption of aboriginal title arises from customary law, it can also be codified nationally by legislation or treaty, and written directly into federal constitutions, as it has been to one degree or another in the aforementioned countries.

While the requirements for establishing aboriginal title may vary from country to country, generally an aboriginal claimant must establish exclusive occupation of the land they are claiming *before* the assertion of colonial sovereignty, and continued occupation to the present day.

Aboriginal title is generally described by lawyers as a "usufruct," which simply means a right to use and manage the land under title, and a right to its economic benefits. However, in practice, *usufruct* may mean anything from a right to use it for specific, enumerated purposes, or a general right to use that approximates ownership just short of "fee simple"—outright private ownership.

Absent knowledge or acceptance of aboriginal title, there is a fundamental assumption that land and resources that are not fee simple are prima facie assumed to be Crown or public property. This creates a problem for both governments and native communities seeking to collaborate in land use and resource stewardship.

In some countries, it was beyond dispute that aboriginal title belonged to native communities before a colonial power acquired or assumed sovereignty over their lands. Indigenous laws preexisted and were assumed to survive the assertion of sovereignty, independent of treaty, executive order, or legislative enactment. But try to tell that to an independent colonial government, or to the European monarch or state that succeeded the one that sent the colonizers to "the New World." Aboriginal title is an uphill battle for any First Nation attempting to claim it.

Once established, however, aboriginal tile is a property right that encompasses the right to use that land for a wide range of purposes, including both aboriginal and modern purposes. And it extends to the exclusive possession, use, and enjoyment of the natural resources attached to the land—minerals, trees, and protein. Aboriginal title also has a significant noneconomic component, as it preserves a relationship of cultural significance between an aboriginal community and its land. So title is directed at the preservation of distinctive aboriginal communities simply by securing their relationship to the lands that sustain them.

Aboriginal title to land is closer to stewardship than ownership, as it assumes a sustainability ethos that prohibits any use of the land that would threaten the food security of the community, while safeguarding the cultural integrity of the land for future generations. Thus, it confirms the right of the aboriginal nation holding title to determine the uses to which the land will be put, which is in essence the right of land management. And it prohibits any use of aboriginal land that would impair its utility for future generations or threaten the bond between aboriginal people and their homeland. For example, strip-mining a hunting ground, putting a golf course on a burial ground, or paving over anything sacred are considered violations of aboriginal title. So is clear-cutting a forest. Only sustainable activity is allowed on aboriginal ground.

* * *

THE FIRST indigenous land rights case under the common law, *Mohegan Indians v. Connecticut*, was litigated from 1705 to 1773, with the British Privy Council rejecting a claim for aboriginal title, noting that "Some tribes are so low in the scale of social organization that their usages and conceptions of rights and duties are not to be reconciled with the institutions or the legal ideas of civilized society. Such a gulf cannot be bridged." This attitude persisted throughout the British Empire for the entire eighteenth century and set the tone for considering aboriginal title in most of Britain's colonies.

Of course, the Haida have never assumed that sovereignty and title were things they had to win or win back. They were rights they had always possessed on Haida Gwaii. Their goal has simply been to establish that fact and have both the nation-state of Canada and the province of British Columbia acknowledge and accept it.

Title and sovereignty are the ultimate quarries of a 250-year worldwide struggle between First Nations and colonists, governments, law courts, media, traders, multinational corporations, and racist intellectuals. They are tightly woven targets on the short lists of a thousand or more indigenous communities seeking some degree of autonomy in at least seventy different countries.

While each of those countries has its own constitution, code of laws, court system, and case laws, there are transferable arguments and customary laws that are respected and effective in many jurisdictions.

7

The Argument

*British Columbia asserts that Haida Gwaii is Crown land,
subject to certain private rights or interest, and subject to
the sovereignty of Her Majesty the Queen and the legislative
jurisdiction of the Parliament of Canada and the Legislature of
the Province of British Columbia.*

Provincial claim for title (2002)

*The Haida Nation asserts that Haida Gwaii is Haida land,
including the water and resources subject to the rights,
sovereignty, ownership, jurisdiction and collective Title of the
Haida Nation who will manage Haida Gwaii in accordance
with its laws, policies, customs and traditions.*

Haida claim for title (2002)

THE BASIC argument for self-determination, sovereignty, and aboriginal title is fairly simple. It's addressed to the colonizer and goes something like this:

We have lived here for a very long time on land we have always assumed was ours. We were here long before you "discovered" us and our homeland, which we have never left. For all this time, we have thrived alone, without foreign assistance, on the resources of our land and water.

Despite the fact that we were secure on lands we stewarded, in a culture we developed, with a religion we owned, under laws and life of our own making, you assumed when you first observed us that we were a bunch of ignorant, heathen savages who had no idea how to manage land, forage and cultivate food, harvest medicines, worship our creator, trade with neighbors, conduct our ceremonies, build homes, create art, or govern ourselves. And you coveted our land, and the resources on and beneath it. So you conquered and subjugated us, and behind the superior firepower of your weapons, you assumed title over our land and sovereignty over us.

You kidnapped and "educated" our children, erased our language, sold our resources to others, extinguished our rights, attempted to convert us to your religion, and turned the best of our rituals into crimes. We eventually asked you to reconsider your actions and the assumptions that informed them. You agreed to do so. Amicably, we negotiated an agreement of understanding, or a governance protocol, a land-use comanagement plan, or a treaty. And amicably you signed it.

But before the ink was dry, you broke it, and returned to confiscating our land and selling our resources to people we had never met. While we are close to giving up the idea of sharing sovereignty with you, we have decided, one last time, to file a claim in your courts, where we seek only what we believe we deserve—self-determination, sovereignty, and aboriginal title to our land; not to some of it, but to all that we say is ours.

And here is how the Haida worded their court claim for aboriginal title, which was filed by the Council of the Haida Nation and its Hereditary Chiefs Council in 2002:

Haida Gwaii is a North American First Nation whose territory includes the land, inland waters, seabed, pelagic waters, air space, in summary everything contained on the 158-island archipelago claimed by the British Crown in 1846 and formalized under the name they had been given by the British explorer who "discovered" them in 1787—the Queen Charlotte Islands, after his Queen, who had never set foot on the islands. Her husband, King George III, had written and signed a Royal Proclamation in 1763. Without our consent and contrary to the principles and accepted practices of the Crown reflected in the King's Proclamation, the Dominion of Canada claimed title and the right to colonize Haida Gwaii.

Prior to 1846 the Haida Nation exclusively occupied Haida Gwaii for at least 10,000 years and have since continued a culture which is based upon the relationship of people to their land, of Haida People to Haida Gwaii. We maintained a spiritual relationship with the beings and the spirits of the earth, the forests, the sea and the sky. We lived within and managed the human use of the entire archipelago. Before and after 1846 we and we alone utilized, conserved and protected the terrestrial and marine ecosystems, to assure the well-being of present and future generations, all in accordance with Haida customs, laws and traditions. We also established trade relationships with other Indigenous Peoples, agents of nation-states, and international trading entities. And we governed Haida Gwaii through the development and maintenance of institutions and laws related to lands and resources, including laws related to access and trespass, which have clearly been violated.

Despite the Crown's disregard of prior title and their efforts to control the resources of Haida Gwaii, the Haida Nation has maintained a substantial connection to the islands through the exercise of political authority and by asserting ownership of Haida Gwaii in dealings with other First Nations, the Crown, and persons authorized by the Crown to engage in industrial and other commercial activities on the islands. We have also developed and maintained institutions to manage our lands and conduct our internal and external affairs.

To the greatest extent possible, the Haida Nation continues to use, harvest, manage and conserve fish and other aquatic species from the sea and inland waters of Haida Gwaii for cultural, domestic and livelihood purposes. We also use, harvest, manage and conserve trees, including old-growth cedar, spruce and hemlock from the forested areas of Haida Gwaii, for cultural, domestic and livelihood purposes. We trade fish and other aquatic species, as well as material goods manufactured from trees harvested from Haida Gwaii, all for commercial purposes, all while managing and conserving our terrestrial and marine ecosystems in accordance with our ancient customs, laws and traditions. We have been very successful at this, as the health and wealth of our nation attests.

The Haida Nation has resisted colonization, and been in constant dispute with the Crown over ownership and jurisdictional matters related to the uses of land and sea. At the same time, we have been ready, willing, and able to enter into good faith negotiations to reach an agreement for coexistence with the Crown, to which we have formally served notice of the continued existence of Haida Title and Rights to Haida Gwaii. We have remained open to seeking appropriate solutions which might harmonize Haida Title and Crown Title, and have entered into comprehensive claims and treaty processes established by the Crown, with a desire to engage in honorable and effective negotiations.[18]

Nevertheless, the Crown has continued to issue tree farm licenses and other harvest permits to extractive industries that compromise our food security through loss of biological diversity and degradation of terrestrial and marine ecosystems throughout the islands. Without consultation or permission the Crown has appropriated our

18 "Haida title" preexists aboriginal title. Some colonial governments respected such title, others did not. And some, like Britain, that did at first, later reversed their position and either extinguished title or simply moved native title holders onto reserves, stole the land, and handed it, fee simple, to settlers from the homeland. It is this tendency the Haida have been facing for two hundred years, and contesting for a century or more.

land and resources, then granted, replaced or renewed tenures to land and resources to transnational corporations from whom it has collected royalties (stumpage, revenues and taxes) while preventing the Haida Nation from receiving financial benefits derived from our own land and resources. The Crown has also prevented, interfered or attempted to prevent and interfere with members of the Haida Nation accessing, using, harvesting, managing, conserving or protecting Haida Gwaii. You have permitted the introduction of nonindigenous species of plants and animals to Haida Gwaii and failed to protect and sustainably manage the resources of the islands, in particular the old-growth forests, watersheds and monumental cedar. All the while, the Crown has denied that we hold Aboriginal Title and has refused or failed to conduct good faith negotiations to reach accommodation.

We are not asking you to give us aboriginal title. We believe we have always owned it. We are merely asking you to recognize that fact.

Since the late fifteenth century, there have been hundreds, if not thousands, of confrontations around the planet between indigenous peoples and explorers, conquerers, imperialists, and other occupying forces. Like the Haida, most First Nations have been seeking a simple affirmation of title, self-determination, and some form of government autonomy. And most of them have failed. Deconstructing their stories on a case-by-case basis indicates that many of them tried some or all of the same tactics the Haida used—blockades, litigation, treaty negotiation, NGO alliances, media campaigns, and lobbying. Their problem wasn't tactics, it was timing, and that has been the brilliance of the Haida—timing.

Badly timed campaigns for anything generally fail or, at best, achieve limited results, even when all the right tactics are employed. Knowing when to move, when to hold back, what to do next, when to strike, and when to strike *forcefully* is something the Haida seem to sense by nature. Although that is not to suggest that Haida elders and chiefs didn't deliberate, argue, and strive for consensus before making every move. They did, endlessly at times. But when they made their move, they did so with an agreement and certainty that the time was right.

And it almost always was.

While the lesson offered by the Haida regarding tactics may or may not be appropriate for one First Nation or another, the lesson of timing should be heeded by them all. Because without good timing, the best tactics can be nothing short of futile. So to expand the formula that is the essence of the Haida struggle for independence…

Well-chosen and well-timed tactics have a better chance to create a winning strategy.

8

The Precedent

*We should regard their determination to be
themselves as a triumph of the human spirit.*

Thomas Berger

THE HAIDA'S case for aboriginal title was preceded and supported by some precedential court rulings and relevant constitutional provisions. Let's start with the case law.

In 1888, a colonial form of aboriginal title was recognized in Canadian common law when the Judicial Committee of the Privy Council (official advisers to the prime minister) in the case of *St. Catherine's Milling v. The Queen*, characterized it as a personal usufruct at the pleasure of the Queen. The Council held that aboriginal title could be taken away at any time.

St. Catherines was more or less the prevailing Canadian case law on aboriginal title until the landmark 1973 Calder decision. In *Calder et al. v. British Columbia*, BC cabinet minister and Nisga'a First Nation chief Frank Arthur Calder, the first Indian to be elected to a Canadian legislature, took the BC government to court in 1967, arguing that aboriginal title to about 2,600 square kilometers of Nisga'a land in and around the Nass River Valley in northwestern BC had never been extinguished, and that aboriginal title was unknown to provincial law and had been extinguished by the Colony of British Columbia before it joined the Canadian Confederation in 1871. Calder and the Nisga'a appealed. Again, the province said there was no such thing as aboriginal title, and if it ever did exist, it had been extinguished. So the case went to the Supreme Court of Canada, where a bizarre split decision launched a protracted land-claims process that continues to this day.

All seven of the Supreme Court's judges in *Calder* agreed that aboriginal title existed. Six of the judges split 3-3 on the question of whether title had been extinguished. The Nisga'a did not prevail because the seventh justice found that the court did not have jurisdiction to make a declaration in favor of the Nisga'a in the absence of a fiat from the lieutenant governor of BC permitting the suit against the provincial government.

Although the court ultimately ruled against the Nisga'a's specific claim, the decision marked the first time any Canadian court acknowledged that aboriginal title to land existed prior to colonization and the Royal Proclamation of 1763. Judges could not agree, however, on whether that title extended to the modern day. So, despite confusion and ambiguity, Calder laid the groundwork for negotiation of a treaty—the Nisga'a Treaty, which would eventually be adopted in 2000. It would be the first contemporary land-claims agreement in British Columbia.

Only four years prior to the *Calder* decision, Canadian Liberal prime minister Pierre Trudeau had rejected aboriginal title outright, saying that the government had no obligation to negotiate treaties with First Nations. "No, we can't recognize aboriginal rights," he proclaimed, "because no society can be built on historical might-have-beens." Trudeau was relying on a 1969 Canadian white paper stating that aboriginal rights "are so general and undefined that it's not realistic to think of them as claims capable of remedy."

After reading the *Calder* decision, Trudeau said, "Perhaps you had more legal rights than we thought you had when we did the white paper." He could see quite clearly that his Supreme Court and his country had taken a giant step toward the recognition of aboriginal title. It was a victory for every First Nation in Canada and encouragement to every First Nation in the world.

In *R. v. Sparrow* (1990), the court for the first time set out criteria for determining whether a right can be considered an "existing" right and whether the government is justified in curtailing such a right. The case stemmed from the 1984 arrest of Ronald Edward Sparrow, a member of the Musqueam band in British Columbia, who was charged with violating fisheries regulations when he used a net that was longer than his fishing license allowed. Sparrow argued that his right to fish with the net was an existing aboriginal right protected by the Canadian Constitution. The court agreed but stipulated that the right is not absolute and can, in certain circumstances, be infringed upon. Like so many aboriginal cases, *Sparrow* was a true but limited victory that has been citied in many native court battles over land and resource rights.

Together, *Calder* and *Sparrow* provided a foundation for future First Nation claims for land title and usufruct rights in Canada. Litigation proceeded. In the treaty the Nisga'a eventually signed with the government, Nisga'a laws take clear precedence over federal or provincial laws. Their case opened the possibility of aboriginal title a little bit wider in Canada. *Delgamuukw v. British Columbia* took it even further.

On December 11, 1997, the Supreme Court of Canada for the first time directly addressed the meaning of *aboriginal title*, clarifying that it meant legal interest in the land itself and the fruits of the land, including minerals beneath it and the forests above it.

The complaint had been filed by Chief Delgamuukw and other hereditary chiefs of the Gitxsan and Wet'suwet'en First Nations in BC. They took the provincial government to the Supreme Court of Canada in an effort to establish ownership and jurisdiction over 58,000 square kilometers (22,000 square miles) of territory in the Skeena watershed in northwestern BC. The court did not rule on the question of ownership, saying the issue had to be decided at a new trial, but they did give a detailed interpretation of what constitutes aboriginal title in Canada, laying out guidelines for how the issue should be approached in future disputes.

Canadian aboriginal title, the court said, is an ancestral right protected by the Constitution (which had been amended in 1982 to include such protections) and relating to land *sui generis*, which, as elsewhere, means there is nothing else quite like it. Aboriginal title is held communally and is distinct from other ancestral rights. It is, therefore, in substance, a right to territory and encompasses exclusive use and occupation. It is not necessary to prove perfect or permanent continuity, said the court; demonstration of a bond between a people and their territory is sufficient, and justices held that oral evidence could be admitted as proof. But they also ruled that aboriginal lands could not be used in a manner that was inconsistent with aboriginal title: if aboriginals wished to use the lands in ways that aboriginal title did not permit, then the lands must be surrendered.

The court also set the criteria for proving title, saying that "in order to make a claim for aboriginal title, the following criteria must be met:

- The land must have been occupied prior to sovereignty.
- If present occupation is relied on as proof of occupation pre-sovereignty, there must be a continuity between present and pre-sovereignty occupation.
- At sovereignty, that occupation must have been exclusive."

The court also stipulated that fee-simple title differs from aboriginal title in three important ways:

- Aboriginal land is communally, not privately or individually, owned.
- Land held pursuant to aboriginal title can be sold only to the government.
- Aboriginal land cannot be used in a way that impairs its utility for traditional use by future generations.

Finally, the court ruled that there is an "inescapable economic aspect" to aboriginal title and that aboriginal communities must be given an opportunity to share in the economic benefits of the land to which they hold title.

Although the justices said they didn't have the evidence they needed to decide if the Gitxsan and Wet'suwet'en held title to the territory they claimed, they did set out rules for what title is and how to prove it. And they distinguished Canadian aboriginal title from any other legal form of ownership:

1. Aboriginal title, like the aboriginals themselves, existed before European settlement and the Crown's declaration of sovereignty. It does not stem from the Crown title like all other forms of legal title in Canada.
2. Aboriginal title is inalienable. It cannot be given or taken away.
3. Aboriginal title is held by all members of an aboriginal nation. It cannot be held by an individual.
4. Aboriginal title is a right to the land itself. It is more than the right to use a certain area. It can compete with other proprietary interests like ownership, leases, and licenses.
5. Aboriginal title can mean exclusive use and occupation. Use can mean any form of activity, including modern economic ones, and is not restricted solely to traditional practices.
6. Aboriginal title can also include mineral rights.
7. Aboriginal title is supposed to protect the relationship between aboriginal people and the land. Because of this, aboriginals cannot use title land for something that will

destroy its traditional value. For example, an area of social or ceremonial significance can't be paved over.

8. Aboriginal title is not absolute. Neither the Crown nor the aboriginal title holder enjoys full or clear title to lands or resources. Each is subject to the other's interest.

The implications of the *Delgamuukw* decision are so monumental that many in the media, in provincial and national politics, and even on First Nations treaty-negotiating teams have not yet fully comprehended how far-reaching its significance is for aboriginal people. It represents an inversion of all of the assumptions and certainties of colonialism. In particular, it provides for the elevation of indigenous legal systems, including systems of land tenure and concepts of sovereignty, to the level of constitutional recognition. The decision also ended long-standing speculation that aboriginal title had been extinguished by colonization or settlement.

While the *Delgamuukw* decision applies only to Canadian First Nations and is enforceable only in Canada, its legal claims and generic arguments are applicable in many other national jurisdictions around the world where aboriginal communities can prove they held exclusive occupation at the time a colonizer asserted sovereignty.

To the majority statement, the chief justice ruling on *Delgamuukw* added these final words: "Ultimately it is through negotiated settlement, with good faith and the give and take on both sides, reinforced by judgments of this court, that we will achieve the reconciliation of preexisting aboriginal sovereignty with the sovereignty of the Crown. Let's face it, we are all here to stay."

When aboriginals were moved onto reserves, the government in power simply assumed title to all land outside the reserves, including hunting and fishing grounds essential to a First Nation's food security. Title to that land was regarded as "extinguished." *Delgamuukw* said no to this argument. The provinces had no right to extinguish title. Aboriginal title existed in both English common law and native customs. So aboriginal title and Crown title coexist, the justices agreed, ruling that the only inherent limit on aboriginal land was use that affected the land's health and productivity for future generations. The court also agreed with Chief Delgamuukw's argument that if the Crown was going to interfere with aboriginal title, it had to do so "honorably" (more on the honor of the Crown to follow). British Columbia responded to the ruling by claiming that it didn't affect the provincial government until title was proven to their satisfaction.

Subsequent decisions have drawn on the fiduciary duty to limit the ways in which the Crown can extinguish aboriginal title, and to require prior consultation where the government has knowledge of a credible, but yet unproven, claim to it. But no case improved the chances for the Haida and other First Nations of Canada to secure aboriginal title more than *Tsilqhot'in Nation v. British Columbia*.

The Tsilhqot'in (pronouced "chil-ko-teen") struggle for title began in 1983, when the province of British Columbia issued a license to Carrier Lumber to cut trees in lands that included a remote central British Columbia territory claimed by the Xeni Gwet'in band of the Tsilhqot'in. The Tsilhqot'in were a seminomadic group of First Nations people who had lived in the area for centuries, managing its lands and repelling invaders. The

Xeni Gwet'in blockaded the area, preventing Carrier from logging and leading to unsuccessful negotiations with the provincial government to continue logging. The Xeni Gwet'in ultimately sought a declaration that would prohibit Carrier's commercial logging operations as well as a claim for aboriginal title.

In 2014, after 339 days of testimony, the Supreme Court, led by Chief Justice Beverly McLachlin, voted unanimously to allow the appeal, thus recognizing the Tsilhqot'in's aboriginal title claim to the 1,750 square kilometers (680 square miles) they had historically occupied. Rejecting the provincial government's claim that aboriginal title applied only to villages and fishing sites, the court instead agreed with the Tsilhqot'in that aboriginal title should extend to the entire traditional territory of an aboriginal group, even if that group was seminomadic and did not create settlements on that territory. It also stated that governments must have consent from First Nations that hold aboriginal title in order to approve developments on their land, and that governments can only override a First Nation's wishes in exceptional circumstances. The court reaffirmed, however, that areas under aboriginal title are not outside the jurisdiction of the provinces, and provincial law still applies.

* * *

CERTAIN SECTIONS of the Canadian Constitution also helped to pave the way for aboriginal title and the Haida case.

In 1982, Canada decided to repatriate its originating constitution, the British North America Act, which was passed in 1867 by the British Parliament, creating the Dominion of Canada. The resulting new Constitution Act of 1982 was brought into force in Ottawa by proclamation of the Queen. Embedded in the act is one very relevant passage, section 35, which "recognizes and affirms existing" aboriginal and treaty rights in Canada. Aboriginal rights protect all activities, practices, and traditions integral to the distinct cultures of First Nations peoples. Treaty rights protect and enforce agreements between them and the Crown. Section 35 also protects aboriginal title, which in turn protects the use of land for traditional practices.

Attached to the new constitution is the Canadian Charter of Rights and Freedoms, a new set of constitutional rights superseding a less powerful and easily amendable statutory Bill of Rights. The charter is intended to protect certain political and civil rights of people in Canada from the policies and actions of all levels of government. Section 25 of the charter addresses aboriginal rights:

> The guarantee in this Charter of certain rights and freedoms shall not be construed as to abrogate or derogate from any aboriginal treaty or other rights or freedoms that pertain to the aboriginal peoples of Canada, including:
>
> (a) any rights or freedoms that have been recognized by the Royal Proclamation of October 7, 1763; and
>
> (b) any rights or freedoms that now exist by way of land claims agreements or may be so acquired.

In other words, the charter must be enforced in a way that does not diminish aboriginal rights.

While a case law is generally only of use to people in the jurisdiction where it was enacted, the arguments, rulings, and principles in all of the above cases are today being cited effectively by First Nations pleading for aboriginal title and sovereignty in the courts of the seventy nation-states where courts exist.

THE PERSISTENCE OF FORCE vs. THE FORCE OF PERSISTENCE

9

The Strategy

We don't use the word claim *because it implies that
we're claiming something that isn't already ours.*

Terri-Lynne Williams, Haida lawyer

THE STORY of Haida resistance begins with their response to
logging. For years, the Haida had been happily trading fish and
furs for medicines and metal tools with visitors from several nations. But when timber companies discovered the extraordinary
size and quality of the old-growth red cedar, yellow cedar, western
hemlock, and Sitka spruce that had evolved on the islands, they
became covetous. Not only was the wood straight-grained, strong,
and clear, the trees grew right down to the water's edge, so could
easily be felled, dragged into the ocean, boomed, and towed to
sawmills on the mainland. And due to superior soil and growing
conditions, trees grow two to three times faster on Haida Gwaii

than they do on the mainland. Thus, the waiting time between first and second cut is shortened.

And when big timber finds a reliable and accessible source of high-grade lumber, they tend to want all of it. Otherwise, their considerable investment in a defined area like Haida Gwaii makes less economic sense. So the trees of Haida Gwaii became highly desirable to a booming global industry—all of them. And as soon as people in the industry realized what existed on Haida Gwaii in the way of wood, half a dozen of the world's largest forestry companies sharpened their chainsaws and headed north.

But instead of going to the Haida to negotiate a tree farm license (TFL), timber companies went five hundred miles south to the Department of Forestry in Victoria, the capital of British Columbia. And because Forestry, not the Haida, would be collecting stumpage for the timber, revenue-hungry bureaucrats happily drew up and granted TFLs to transnational corporations like Weyerhaeuser, MacMillan Bloedel, Rayonier, Brascan, and Western Forest Products, whose senior executives had never set foot on the islands and didn't speak a word of Haida.

Logging on Haida Gwaii began in earnest in 1901, when the islands were at their most vulnerable, having lost most of their population to smallpox. For the first few decades, Sitka spruce (*Picea sitchensis*) was the most desired tree, as its stiffness-to-weight ratio made it ideal in the early days for ships and their masts, then later for light-framed military aircraft, and still today for string instrument soundboards. But for the first half of the twentieth century, it was a fairly low-volume harvest for the logging companies, who employed just enough Haida people to keep the native population from protesting too loudly. But by the midcentury, the pace of extraction began to pick up. And so did Canada's oppression of its native people, who were virtually powerless to resist the loss of communal lands, assimilation, and the exploitation of their resources. The potlatch and sun dance were still illegal, and native Canadians had yet to receive the right to vote. Canada's aboriginal communities had declared themselves "First Nations," but it was only a name. In actuality, they remained essentially powerless to stop the erosion of their rights and the theft of natural resources they had survived on for thousands of years.

Talunkwan, a small island nestled on the eastern shore off Moresby, southernmost of the two largest islands of Haida Gwaii, was first to be clear-cut, and its clearly visible devastation—in the form of erosion, landslides, and sedimentation of salmon streams—became a worldwide symbol of excessive forestry, a monument to the ecological destruction of clear-cut logging. Ugly photos sparked an insurrection that spread to every corner of the province and eventually spawned anti-logging movements and BC timber boycotts the world over. *Talunkwanization* became a noun in the movement.

The Gowgaia Institute, a Vancouver-based research project created by Earthlife Canada, estimated that 50 million cubic meters of high-value timber was logged from 420,000 acres of Haida Gwaii in the twenty-five years between 1979 and 2004. Ninety-five percent of that harvest left the island as unmilled raw lumber worth $20 billion on the open market, $2 billion of which went as stumpage to the province, not the Haida. No wonder Haida people regarded the government of British Columbia as a money-grubber no different than big timber. During that period, forestry did account for 36 percent of income on the islands, but most of that went to corporate foresters from the mainland, not to the Haida, who were systematically excluded from managerial or entrepreneurial roles within the industry.[19]

As they watched their precious timber being stripped away, barge load by barge load, and with it their only hope for wealth and independence, Haida leaders began to realize that they had to take a stand, and that they were up against at least three formidable foes—big timber, the province of British Columbia, and the Dominion of Canada. It was only through a strategic combination of tactics and timing that they were able to do what they did.

Affirming a Nation

THE HAIDA have always regarded the 158 islands of Haida Gwaii as a nation, a First Nation, thousands of years old, arbitrarily and illegally absorbed under threat of force into an imperious Second Nation. In order to gain the respect of the Second Nation, and the rest of the world, it seemed worthwhile to Haida leaders to make their ancient and well-governed civilization look more legitimate in the eyes of the Second Nation, which is to say, more European than native. So on December 7, 1974, they formed the Council of the Haida Nation (CHN) and declared it "the rightful heir and owner of Haida Gwaii" with a vision to organize a somewhat disparate collection of bands, villages, and settlements into one political entity with one border, one language, one origin, and one people. It was a bold move that challenged all legislation defining power and sovereignty in the Dominion of Canada. The founding convention gave the CHN "complete authority to represent the Haida people in discussion, negotiation or litigation

19 Second to forestry as an income source on the islands was the public sector at 30 percent, followed by transfer payments at 13 percent, tourism at 5 percent, and fishing and trapping at 4 percent.

with or against all governments, domestic or foreign, as well as corporations and other organizations affecting the Haida people."

As an organized nation, with all the declarations and institutions of a nation-state, the Haida believed they would appear more respectable, more credible, to their occupiers, with whom it would thereby be easier to share sovereignty. They also hoped it would be easier to have Haida title recognized in law and ensure Haida participation in all social, political, and economic development affecting the islands and their people.

Given that the struggle for sovereignty on Haida Gwaii was against subordination to a dominant society and to the multinational corporate takeover of their resources, the declaration creating the CHN quite appropriately begins with these sentiments:

> Be it resolved that this Convention directs the Executives in the formulation of a proposal for negotiating a land settlement. Executives should seek the formalization and retention of aboriginal title rather than the surrender of their aboriginal rights forever.

With that mandate, the CHN became the national government of Haida Gwaii and the Haida people.

Framing a Constitution

THE NEXT step toward sovereignty was to draft a constitution, a process which began in 1980. It took Haida leaders almost twenty-five years to debate, draft, and ratify their constitution (it wasn't fully adopted until 2003). But as always, patience was a virtue that came naturally to a ten-thousand-year-old civilization that had for two centuries been living under a constitution designed for the dominion that governed them, a document that in turn mimicked Britain's constitution, which protected the interests of an empire and made absolutely no mention of land or sea or the people's relationship to them. Unlike most national constitutions, Haida Gwaii's created a binding legal mandate granting solid constitutional rights to nature and the natural environment. It directs the CHN to "establish land and resource policies consistent with Nature's ability to produce," and goes on from there to say

> Our physical and spiritual relationship with the lands and waters of Haida Gwaii, our history of coexistence with all living things over thousands of years is what makes up Haida culture. *Yah'guudang*—our respect for all living things—celebrates the way our lives and spirits are intertwined and honors the responsibility we hold to future generations… The fate of our culture runs parallel with the fate of the oceans, sky and forest people.

Attached to the Haida Constitution is a list of "Mandates and Responsibilities" that empowers and directs the CHN to protect Haida heritage and cultural identity, promote peaceful coexistence with other governments, establish election procedures, regulate commerce, and protect the foreign interests of Haida Gwaii. But perhaps the most essential order to the CHN is to strive for "full independence, sovereignty and self-sufficiency." I asked a former president of the Haida Nation, who drafted that clause, if it called for secession from Canada. He assured me it did not. "We intend to remain part of Canada and British Columbia," he said. "We simply want to make our decisions independent of them both."

By creating a constitution, not unlike that of Canada, the Haida have established themselves as something close to a modern democratic state, respectful of modern law. And they have proved to skeptics that they can govern themselves. That doesn't mean they have forsaken their traditional forms of governance, their community structure, or their deepest values. They have simply formalized them into a working document and called it their constitution. (For the full text of the Haida Constitution, see appendix 4.)

While the Haida resisted colonization and protested the Crown's extinguishing their title, taking their land, and giving resources to third parties, they have always been open to harmonizing Crown and aboriginal title and sharing sovereignty with Ottawa (the capital of Canada) and Victoria (the capital of British Columbia). And they have never demanded fee-simple title over private land on the islands, much of which is owned by non-Haida people. Their complaint has always been about the way federal and provincial governments gave exclusive use of their land to outsiders.

In 1981, the CHN submitted a land claim to the federal government in Ottawa. But Ottawa would not consider it unless British Columbia was at the table. No sooner than they'd taken their seats, BC officials refused to surrender any semblance of title to Crown land. That same year, the CHN also issued a statement calling for a 50 percent reduction of logging on Haida Gwaii. A new battle began.

Protecting History

FORESTRY WAS considered a major economic driver in British Columbia. It was a reliable, fast-growing source of revenue for the government agencies that reaped the benefits, and they were more than happy to keep it coming.

In 1978, the BC provincial government sold a tree farm license on Lyell Island to Rayonier Incorporated of Jacksonville, Florida. In 1979, Haida Gwaii petitioned for locally owned TFLs and called for a hearing on the removal of Rayonier's license. By the turn of the decade, Rayonier, Weyerhaeuser, and other logging giants had clear-cut huge swaths of Graham Island, the largest island on the archipelago, and most of the northern forests in South Moresby. And they were moving south. In their path were scores of vacant Haida villages abandoned during the nineteenth-century smallpox epidemic. Next to each village was a mass grave of ancestors stricken with the disease.[20] Disturbance of the salmon streams was bad enough—disturbing sacred sites was unacceptable. Pierre Berton, one of Canada's most prolific and popular pundits, described clear-cut logging on Haida Gwaii as "an act of vandalism… and a national disgrace." It was time to take a stand, time to block roads. "Enough is enough" became the rallying cry for a blockade of the logging road to Athlii Gwaii (aka Lyell Island), next in line for clear-cutting.

One brilliant tactic the Haida used was to find and record the location of every "culturally modified tree" (CMT) on the

20 In one of the world's most egregious acts of cultural vandalism, many of those graveyards were dug up by anthropologists, who carried skeletal remains off to museums and DNA labs for genetic screening. A small group of Haida have since traveled the world politely asking scientists and museum directors to return their ancestors, and in some cases have succeeded in bringing them home. The Field Museum of Natural History in Chicago, which had stored the Haida bones in sterile basement vaults for almost a century, not only paid to have the intact remains of close to 150 people shipped back to Haida Gwaii, but also picked up the airfare of the Haida Repatriation Committee members who had flown to Chicago to ask for them. At home, the remains were ceremoniously laid to rest once again, in the forests where their people were born and where they belonged.

islands. CMTs are trees that were marked or altered in some way by ancient Haida carvers and boatbuilders, modified in ways that served cultural or practical purposes. Core samples would be taken from tall spruce and cedars to see if their wood was suitable for canoes and longhouse beams. If not, the trees would be left to grow on, permanently modified by the Haida. The trees, according to contemporary Haida, are not only sacred artifacts; they are living and carbon-dateable evidence that the islands were occupied and used hundreds, even thousands, of years ago.

"Every tree utilized by our people tells us something of their history and movement," explained the president of the Haida Nation. "Every tree removed erases traces of their existence." CMTs became the *bête noire* of multinational foresters as their very existence has put huge tracts of forest off-limits to logging. And they have simultaneously been used to prove Haida occupancy of the islands for centuries before the arrival of Europeans, a prerequisite to establishing aboriginal title. (See sidebar on the advantages of mapping culturally significant sites, page 42.)

A War in the Woods
DURING THE 1980s, a powerful, internationally driven anti-logging campaign began heating up in British Columbia. By the middle of the decade, "the war in the woods" was in full swing and was drawing environmental activists from around the world. A boycott of BC west coast lumber was launched in Europe. In 1983, the South Moresby Resource Planning Team, a collaborative government/native project, recommended placing 95 percent of the remaining area of Moresby Island off-limits to

all development. Western Forest Products didn't blink and continued logging on Lyell Island.

In 1985, an ad hoc committee of Haida and environmentalists calling itself the Island Protection Society (IPS) was formed. Immediately upon its launch, IPS filed a formal request that the rest of South Moresby be set aside and put off-limits to future logging. Soon thereafter, IPS published a stunning coffee-table book entitled *Islands at the Edge: Preserving the Queen Charlotte Islands Wilderness*, which became an illustrated manifesto to declare the unlogged portion of South Moresby a "protected wilderness area." (For more about *Islands at the Edge*, and the value of well-illustrated coffee-table books, see sidebar on page 101.)

Concurrent with the book launch, IPS and the Haida began a blockade of Lyell Island. All logging roads on the island were shut down by Haida protesters. Western Forest Products then filed for an injunction against the Haida, which was granted. The Haida ignored the court order and brought their elders to the blockade. Seventy-two were arrested. The elders went first, among them eleven who were flown by helicopter to Prince Rupert on the mainland and charged with criminal contempt and "mischief."[21] But more elders headed south to take their places, and the blockade continued. TV newscasts carried dramatic footage of elders draped in ceremonial red-and-black button jackets being led away from the blockade in handcuffs. Sympathy for the Haida and support for a wilderness preserve on South Moresby became national passions across Canada.

21 Section 387.1 of the Canadian Criminal Code reads: "Anyone commits mischief who willfully destroys or damages property; renders property dangerous, useless, inoperative or ineffective; obstructs or interrupts or interferes with the lawful use, enjoyment or operation of property."

"This is our land, and we are definitely not afraid of going to jail," one elder told the media, which by then was giving the blockade daily coverage. "For what?" she asked. "For protecting our land?"

"They bring dignity to what we are doing," declared a younger protester, whose grandmother had been arrested the day before.

It was working. Loggers could not get to work and were not about to push old ladies into the ditch to do so. A simultaneous pro-Haida protest was launched in Victoria, and the national campaign for a protected wilderness area in South Moresby heated up. Meanwhile, strong opposition to the Haida surfaced in the form of a colorful weekly newspaper called the *Red Neck News*, the acerbic editor of which opined that the blockade was being driven by "American hippy draft dodgers" with "no background in forestry or economics." They and environmentalists and the Haida were "hurting the working man" with their "instant money" and "outrageous lies."

Stimulated by that message—and dismayed by the anti-logging campaign, the plan to create a national park in

The Power and Effect of One Book

Everything depends on everything else.
Haida wisdom

THE ROLE and value of a well-written, powerfully illustrated coffee-table book about a place or region in trouble is inestimable— the Sierra Club expanded its global membership exponentially after publishing a series of them. If done right, these books inspire, they inform, and they motivate, and if used as the Haida used *Islands at the Edge*, they become a powerful tool and tactic in a larger strategy to save a place and protect a culture.

Like so many things that were done during the Haida struggle for sovereignty, the timing of this book's release was perfect. The South Moresby wilderness protection "lobby" was in Ottawa pressing politicians and bureaucrats to create a national park in South Moresby; a caravan of supporters was crossing the country; and David Suzuki was on every other TV network lyrically singing the praises of Gwaii Haanas, the park, and the people who would own and comanage South Moresby, and the Haida's opposition to granting new tree farm licenses to corporate foresters—local non-Haida loggers and anti-environmentalists formed an organization called Share the Rock (STR). In one of his many mischievous moves, the president of Haida Gwaii joined the organization and opened a cordial dialogue with its founders. Somehow, he managed to persuade STR that the so-called falldown effect would eventually put them all out of work. The falldown effect measures the decline in timber supply between old growth and second growth. At current logging rates, the president told the loggers, all harvestable timber would be gone completely by 2027 and would not recover for twenty years.

STR leaders could see the consequences. They would be out of work in twenty years. So they disbanded, requested intervenor status on behalf of the Haida, and released a "Unity Statement" recognizing Haida Gwaii as the hereditary homeland of the Haida people. And the *Red Neck News* suspended publication. Upon signing the statement for the Haida, one hereditary chief said, "Today, the people of Haida Gwaii walked together." By that he meant native and nonnative residents had joined hands to fight industry and government together, something that has rarely happened anywhere in the world.

Sharing Power

IN 1986, new logging permits were granted and others extended on Lyell Island. More blockades were planned, but before they were launched, the Haida built a traditional longhouse at Windy Bay and invited the loggers and their families to a feast. They came, and a long reconciliation process began. Later that year, the province announced a moratorium on new permits in South Moresby, and the CHN and Canada began to consider the creation of a national park in the unlogged southern reaches of the archipelago that would be managed cooperatively by the Haida and the Canadian government.

Meanwhile, in Ottawa, the Federal Department of Justice became deeply concerned about a "Statement of Purpose" for South Moresby drafted by the Haida, in it. This book helped make it happen.

Anyone anywhere in the world who spent an hour with *Islands at the Edge* would be motivated to visit the southern reaches of Haida Gwaii as soon as possible, and if they did so, they would arrive sympathetic to the Haida's desire to stop the ravaging of their homeland and establish autonomy over some of the most remarkable islands on the planet.

which mention was made of "hereditary activities," "a vital part of our spiritual and ancestral home," and "our right to continue traditional activities." Justice lawyers feared that sentences like that might "compromise land-claims negotiations." All copies of the report containing those sentiments were shredded, and the comanagement agreement that was proposed for the area never mentioned "aboriginal title" or "traditional activities." The Canadian federal government seemed to agree that a national wilderness area should be created in South Moresby, but only on their terms. The Haida opposed it.

"We didn't stand on the line to have a national park shoved down our throat," remarked the president of the Haida Nation. "Our objective, preservation, has been won. It's *our* responsibility to manage South Moresby. Anything Parks Canada does should be with our consent."

Shortly after he said that, the president declined the governor general of Canada's Conservation Award for his part in saving South Moresby. "I can't accept this award until the Haida feel at home in Canada," he said. The way the federal government wanted to shift responsibility from Victoria to Ottawa he saw as simply "another erosion of title," and demanded equal say in everything regarding the management of South Moresby, park or no park.

"Whose land do you think you're standing on?" he asked one federal bureaucrat touring the area. He and five other Haida leaders later renounced their citizenship of Canada and tore up their passports. They weren't seceding from Canada, they wanted the government to know, simply reacting to a serious breakdown in the rule of law. "You are not behaving right or legally," the president told a federal official.

The Haida then told the federal Parks Canada bureaucrats in Ottawa that if they didn't approve the creation of a comanaged national park on South Moresby, the CHN was prepared to ask the province to create and comanage a park. Since BC had already created provincial parks on the islands, the Haida were confident they would consider their request for one more, despite the fact that the minister of forests and other Victoria bureaucrats opposed the idea.

In 1988, Canada and Haida Gwaii agreed in principle to create the South Moresby National Park Reserve and name it Gwaii Haanas, but until the conflicts over rights and title were settled, the CHN refused to open the park, even after Canada committed $106 million to the project and $38 million to a regional economic development fund named the Gwaii Trust, including $12 million that was committed to the South Moresby Forest Replacement Account for sustainable forest management on the islands. Loggers who were looking forward to more work on South Moresby were told that they had been given "a day off" that would last forever.

In 1993, following five more years of intense negotiation, the Gwaii Haanas Agreement was signed between Haida Gwaii and Canada, creating the Archipelago Management Board. The board has three federal officials and three Haida, with one independent tiebreaker. Together, they manage the three-part Gwaii Haanas National Park Reserve, National Marine Conservation Reserve, and Haida Heritage Site. Gwaii Haanas is today regarded as one of the most unique national parks in the world, and was almost immediately declared best national park in the world by *Condé Nast Traveller*. Unlike most of the others, it is a true wilderness area, with no roads, no trails, no concessions, and only one very small resort—a former whaling station, totally off the grid and offering rustic rooms and home-cooked meals for the few intrepid explorers who make it to the southern tip of the park.

The power-sharing agreement between Canada and Haida Gwaii regards Gwaii Haanas as two separate and distinct land designations, one as a national park and the other a heritage site. While Canada regards the park as its own and the Haida regard the heritage site as theirs, the comanagement arrangement appears to be working. The tiebreaker on the management board has yet to be called into action.

Residing at each of five long-abandoned Haida villages is a Haida watchman, one per village. They are there to protect the villages from archaeological plunder (which has over the years been a huge problem on the islands) and to recount the history of the place to visitors, limited to twelve at a time, most of whom arrive by sailboats, kayaks, and the occasional float plane. One of the villages, Ninstints, has been declared a UNESCO World Heritage Site. National park enthusiasts and officials travel to Gwaii Haanas from around the world for design and management advice. And so do indigenous people, though they are less likely to have been inspired by the design or management of the park than by the words of the Haida president upon signing the Gwaii Haanas Agreement with Canada and the province.

"What we are celebrating here today," he said, "is that Canada first, and then BC, accepted Haida law and brought their laws in line with ours. People need to understand that we weren't protesting [when we barricaded these islands], we were upholding our own laws. Haida Gwaii is Haida land, always has been, always will be." He was reminding his people and the rest of the world that long before Canada created a national park on South Moresby, the CHN had designated it a Haida Heritage Site, and that the unique agreement between Canada and the CHN was based on the Haida's assertion of title.

It's also important for other First Nations around the world to note the distinction between comanagement and shared jurisdiction. Under comanagement, decision-making is delegated. Under shared jurisdiction, regimes like the Gwaii Haanas Agreement, two equal parties share decision-making. Shared jurisdiction between nation-states and aboriginal communities remains rare around the world, as negotiated power sharing is aggressively resisted by national and provincial governments whenever it is proposed, and governments rarely share power with indigenous peoples unless they are ordered to do so by a court of law.

Of course, this unique landmark agreement didn't just happen. It was forced upon a powerful national government by the resolve, patience, and strategic brilliance of a small community of people tirelessly asserting aboriginal title and the basic human right to self-determination. (For more about Gwaii Haanas National Park, see sidebar on page 109.)

Going to Court

"BLOCKADES DON'T work by themselves," a former president of the Haida Nation remarked. "There needs to be a legal strategy. But a legal strategy won't work by itself either. We had the courts, our alliances, and blockades all working together while we developed and negotiated a land-use plan. Timing was always at the forefront of our minds, and our timing was good."

If it's the state that is granting permission to extractive corporations to mine or harvest resources from your land, then the state must be your target as well as the corporation. But where and when to challenge the state becomes the central strategic question. The *where* is likely in the state's own courts, but that only works if their courts have enough power, enough authority, that political leaders and corporate executives will abide by the courts' rulings. That is the case in Canada, but by no means everywhere in the world. The *when* is the all-important question that requires as much deliberation, skill, and talent as preparing your case for court.

One aspect of their strategy that the Haida emphasize is carefully assessing the politics of the government you are dealing with, because where the majority of a legislature or a cabinet stands on economic and social issues will inform your strategy. Throughout the Haida's long struggle with the province, British Columbia's politics have swung wildly from right to left and back again. As the premier and legislature shifted suddenly from pro-business to pro-union, and from pro- to anti-environment, the Haida had to shift their strategy, sometimes waiting for the election of a more sympathetic majority, or even longer for courts with more respect for aboriginal rights and sovereignty.

For almost a decade, the Haida wanted TFL 39, the tree farm license awarded to Western Forest Products, quashed. This was no small item as the license covered one-quarter of the land base of Haida Gwaii and logging in the area had exceeded sustainable rates for years. But the BC court told them they would have to prove title before they could summarily quash it themselves. So in March 2002, the Haida Nation filed a case with the Supreme

Court of Canada asserting aboriginal rights and title to the land, inland waters, seabed, and sea of Haida Gwaii. They also demanded compensation for "profits, taxes, stumpage, and royalty fees paid to the province," and the withdrawal of "all forestry, mineral, and other permits and licenses" on the islands. The court was also asked to decide whether or not the province was required to consult with the Haida Nation before granting new TFLs or other extraction permits to off-island interests.

In court, aligned against the Haida with Weyerhaeuser and big timber were the governments of British Columbia, Alberta, Saskatchewan, Ontario, Quebec, and Nova Scotia, alongside the Business Council of British Columbia, the Cattlemen's Association, and several mining companies. In a jointly signed brief, these "friends of the court" argued that economies would fail and livelihoods would be ruined if they were required to consult with

Gwaii Haanas

THERE ARE currently over 120,000 officially protected areas scattered about the world. Together, they cover a land mass larger than the entire continent of Africa and include nature reserves, national parks, wilderness areas, marine sanctuaries, protected habitats, and community-based conservation areas. They all differ in some respects, but none so much as the Gwaii Haanas National Marine Conservation Reserve and Haida Heritage Site, on the southern reaches of the Haida Gwaii archipelago, which is without doubt the most creative and unusual protected area on the planet.

One of the many ways that Gwaii Haanas is

unique is that its creation did not displace or evict indigenous people, as that of so many other protected areas did. In fact, quite the contrary. By asserting aboriginal title to the land and sea that comprise the park and marine reserve, and creating a heritage site at the same location before negotiations began on the park, the Haida were able to not only remain on the land but also share jurisdiction over it with the government of Canada.

A calm day on Haida Gwaii is a rare event. It's a place better known for its ferocious winds and turbulent waters. But despite the weather, even in torrential rains and howling storms, the place is compelling and attracts ecotourists and wildlife biologists from around the world.

Although it is officially a national park, Gwaii

the Haida before proceeding with their work on Haida Gwaii.

One of the wisest things the Haida have done is to send one of their own through law school, and, once accredited, to send her back to Ottawa to press the Supreme Court for title. "The cedar tree is our sister," a tall and striking Terri-Lynne Williams told the seven justices before her, "providing for and sustaining our culture." Co-counsel Louise Mandell would later comment on the tremendous advantage of having a Haida lawyer, rather than herself, argue this landmark case:

I don't think the court ever had the facts rendered the way she presented them... from a Haida perspective. I couldn't do that. I'm not aboriginal. Terri was able to refer to her client, the Haida, her own people, in a personal sense, as in "I" and "we" and "our," and render the facts from her perspective rather than the way the court is used to. It was a first-time beautiful moment for advocacy, to see an aboriginal attorney speaking about their own rights, their own territory, and their own people, attempting as counsel to persuade the court to see it from their perspective.

As the Haida awaited a decision from Ottawa, the province of British Columbia stepped forward and offered to release 20 percent of Haida Gwaii to the Haida, in the form of protected areas. In return, the Haida were to relinquish title to the rest of the archipelago. The president of the CHN dismissed the offer as "mischief… They are not offering us 20 percent of their land," he said. "They are asking us to give them 80 percent of our land… Our people come from every part of these islands. There is no place we can give up." The Haida ignored the provincial offer and initiated a "Community Planning Forum" with industry leaders, the province, and island communities.

Haanas is really more of a wilderness area, wild land and wild water, no roads and no trails through a virtually impenetrable forest. There are places to camp along the eastern shoreline, but access to the interior of the park is only for the hardiest bushwhackers. And the western coast, which rises dramatically from a sheer 9,000-foot submarine cliff to 3,000-foot snow-capped mountains, is about as hostile and treacherous as any shoreline in the world.

The wildlife within the boundaries of Gwaii Haanas is as diverse and bountiful as anywhere on Earth, even more so than the Galapagos, which is no doubt why Haida Gwaii is known to the endless swarm of wildlife biologists who visit and study there as "the Galapagos of the North." Many species are endemic to Haida Gwaii, among them are a distinctive subspecies of saw-whet owl, hairy woodpecker, Steller's jay, and Peale's peregrine falcon. Eleven species of mammals are native to Gwaii Haanas: the largest black bear in the world, the pine marten, river otter, Haida ermine, dusky shrew, silver-haired bat, California myotis, Keen's myotis, little brown bat, and deer mouse. The eleventh species, once plentiful on the islands, the Dawson caribou, was hunted to extinction by settlers in 1908. Approximately 1.5 million seabirds from twelve species nest on the islands, including the ancient murrelet, a species at risk, for which Haida Gwaii is the only nesting location in Canada. Cassin's auklets and rhinocerus auklets also nest in globally significant populations. Haida Gwaii is known for its storm petrels and pigeon guillemots.

Discussions went on for eighteen months, two to three days per meeting. The purpose of the meetings was to address power imbalances on the islands and decide how power should work there in the future. Twenty-nine people participated, representing fifteen different interests and sectors. Nine of the delegates were Haida. In over forty full days of public meetings, topics ranged from protected areas, to old-growth retention, ecosystem integrity, spiritual and cultural values, economic well-being, cedar, tourism, and community.

Also running concurrent to the Supreme Court's deliberations was an event in Vancouver, BC, billed as the Turning Point Conference. Thirteen Pacific coastal First Nations, including the Haida, met and signed a declaration which read in part, "The connection of land and sea with the people has given rise to our ancient northwest cultures. The life force [of this region] is under threat like never before, and all people must be held accountable."[22] The Turning Point Declaration eventually led to the protection of the Great Bear Rainforest (GBR), the lush, temperate forest that borders the entire coast of British Columbia. It also gave rise to a new coalition called Coastal First Nations (CFN), which remains a powerful negotiating forum for the Haida and their neighbors on the Pacific coast. CFN regards itself as the ultimate guardians of the GBR.

Twenty-nine species of marine mammals inhabit the surrounding waters, including twenty-three species of whales, three dolphins species, two porpoise species, and the largest colony of Steller's sea lions on Canada's west coast. The sea otter was once plentiful but was hunted to local extinction. They are slowly returning. And there are more than 6,800 species of flora and fauna on the archipelago.

Gwaii Haanas is managed cooperatively by the Archipelago Management Board (AMB), which is comprised of three Haida representatives, three Canadian government officials, and a seventh independent tiebreaker. AMB works on a consensus-based decision-making model.

22 Here is the full Turning Point Declaration:
PREAMBLE
The North Pacific Coast is a rich, varied and fragile part of the natural world. The connection of land and sea with people has given rise to our ancient northwest cultures.
We recognize this life source is under threat like never before and that all people must be held accountable. This united declaration is the foundation for protecting and restoring our culture and the natural world.
We are the ones that will live with the consequences of any actions that take place in our territories.
DECLARATION
We declare our life source is vital to the sustenance and livelihood of our culture and our very existence as a people.
The First Nations of the North Pacific inherit the responsibility to protect and restore our lands, water and air for future generations.
We commit ourselves:
• To making decisions that ensure the well-being of our lands and waters.
• To preserving and renewing our territories and cultures through our tradition, knowledge
and authority.
• To be honest with each other and respectful of all life.
We will support each other and work together as the original people of the North Pacific Coast, standing together to fulfill these commitments.
Signed by thirteen First Nations and councils, this 13th day of June 2000.

In June 2003, the federal and provincial governments filed separate counterstatements to the 2002 Haida title case. Both argued that the Haida's case was "baseless" and should be dismissed. Both said that the Council of the Haida Nation had no valid claim to the islands. The provincial government even denied the existence of a Haida Nation, and despite convincing archaeological evidence to the contrary, said that prior to 1846 the islands were never occupied or possessed communally and exclusively by a single unified aboriginal group. The province did admit that people who all spoke the Haida language lived on the islands at the time of European contact, but they "lived in small autonomous family groups which were widely dispersed and not politically unified or organized." As if it were some mere coincidence of nature that they spoke the same language. The federal government did recognize the Haida Nation's existence, but denied it had claim to the islands.

Title, both governments argued, could only be claimed by an individual village "or resource-gathering site held by an autonomous kin group… rather than the Haida Nation as a whole." And title, they said, could "never [be] extended to the whole of the Claim Area." Allowing title to individual native settlements—"small spots"—while denying it to hunting grounds, fisheries, and intervillage space, has been a common practice of imperial governments throughout the world. The Haida contested the idea, on Haida Gwaii and everywhere else, and they are committed to the principle that the land and water between settlements is as vital to island and forests peoples' livelihoods as their homes and villages, and thereby deserve to be included under aboriginal title.

Both governments, in Ottawa and Victoria, also argued that "because the original inhabitants of [so many of] these villages abandoned them long ago, their descendants lost any claim to these lands." Virtually none of the vacant villages on Haida Gwaii were "abandoned"; their entire populations were wiped out suddenly by smallpox. There are mass graves of rapidly buried victims to prove that at most of the village sites, which were never resettled for fear that the virus was still there.

Both federal and provincial governments claimed a legal right to control *all* resources on the islands, and argued that the Haida people have suffered no hardships as a consequence of their extraction, or of related government actions. "Further, the Plaintiffs have, instead of bringing suit in a timely fashion, slept on their alleged rights"—i.e., they were late.

The province argued that any financial claims "must be against the federal government, because all aboriginal peoples are wards of the Crown, and any responsibility of the Crown to provide for the welfare and protection of native peoples is, as a matter of constitutional law, fundamentally an obligation of the Crown." (The provincial government of British Columbia has no problem describing itself as "the Crown" when it has need to flex its power.) The federal government disagreed, saying that the province was liable because it received all financial benefits (stumpage) from the extraction of resources on the islands.

For two long years, the Haida assumed that both governments were deaf to their oral traditions and blind to their archaeological ruins, thanks to the country's and province's disregard of overwhelming evidence that the Haida people had hunted, fished, and cultivated the land, water, and resources of Haida Gwaii for thousands of years. Canada and its westernmost province were, in effect, refusing to recognize the very existence of a unique and productive civilization, and to acknowledge the resilience, knowledge, capabilities, and expertise that qualified the Haida to manage their own land and govern their own nation.

Then, on November 18, 2004, when the Haida truly believed that Ottawa had abandoned them, the Supreme Court of Canada handed down a surprising judgment in *Haida Nation v. British Columbia*, ruling unanimously (7-0) that the province must consult with the Haida before issuing tree farm licenses (or, for that matter, *any* extractive licenses). "Put simply, Canada's aboriginal peoples were here when Europeans came, and were never conquered," wrote Chief Justice Beverly McLachlan. "Honourable negotiation implies a duty to consult with Aboriginal claimants and conclude an honourable agreement reflecting the claimants' inherent rights… Where the government has knowledge of an asserted Aboriginal right or title, it must consult the Aboriginal peoples on how the exploitation of the land should proceed."

And McLachlan admonished the province for presenting "an impoverished vision of the honour of the Crown. The Crown, acting honourably, cannot cavalierly run roughshod over Aboriginal interests where claims affecting these interests are being seriously pursued in the process of treaty negotiation and proof… When the distant goal of proof is finally reached, the Aboriginal peoples may find their land and resources changed and denuded. This is not reconciliation. Nor is it honourable."

Terri-Lynne Williams couldn't have worded that opinion better herself. One First Nation chief commended her work and described the outcome as "a tremendous victory felt throughout the indigenous world."

Making Allies

ENCOURAGED BY the Supreme Court ruling, the Council of the Haida Nation returned to crafting a vision for land-use planning based on what they called "ecosystem-based management," which relies largely on the "traditional ecological knowledge" (TEK) passed orally from generation to generation in most native cultures of the world. In the Haida's ecosystem, TEK is focused primarily on the obvious connection between forests, salmon, and bears. From that relationship arose the Haida Land Use Vision statement of 2004, the essence of which reads, "The land and waters of Haida Gwaii can and must be made well again. Our economic needs can and must be brought into balance with the capacity of the land to function and provide. We have the political will and we accept the responsibility to see that this is done." They called it Haida LUV, and it became the basis for land-use planning on the islands and for negotiations with both federal and provincial governments. (See appendix 3 for the full Haida LUV statement.)

It had been twenty years since the first Haida blockade on Lyell Island, and the Haida truly believed that they had earned the courtesy of consultation before new logging permits could be granted on the islands. But without warning, Weyerhaeuser sold TFL 39 to another logging company, and the province did nothing to stop the transfer. Renewed clear-cutting on Graham Island seemed imminent. It was time to strike again. Meetings were held and tactics considered. High on the list was civil disobedience.

"We were really losing patience," one leader recalls. "We looked at all the options, even armed confrontation. But we knew if we did that we'd be beat. We were outgunned. And we knew there were lots of people in government who would have liked nothing better than for us to make an armed blockade, and just done away with us." So once again, a warrior tribe opted for peaceful protest.

Launching a blockade is not an easy decision. It has to be justified and have a reasonable expectation of success. Otherwise, it risks becoming a costly and futile gesture, which inevitably engenders bad media and bad public relations. On March 22, 2005, the barricades went up and "Islands' Spirit Rising" was under way. The old "Enough is Enough" and "The Crown has no honour" banners were visible again, and the cameras were rolling. At one point, the Haida seized and claimed ownership of five to ten million dollars' worth of felled logs in response to Weyerhaeuser's breach of their contract. They threatened to sell the logs to support community projects.

But there was concern among the Haida that nonnative residents were becoming uneasy about their future on the islands and concerned about whether or not the government had their best interests in mind. They had nothing to fear, assured the president of the Haida Council. "We've been fighting governments all these years," he said. "Now we are working alongside you, and we are going to do what we can to make it work. You have worked beside us. Our kids go to school together. This is about better management of the land."

Non-Haida islanders, even loggers, gradually joined the Haida and acknowledged that the forests were in better hands with them than the province and the corporations they had favored for so long. Of Weyerhaeuser's 155 employees on the islands, 135 crossed the line. "I'm on the Haida side now," declared one logger. Weyerhaeuser wives held their own protest, against the export of Haida Gwaii logs to the US. "Weyerhaeuser is a community wrecker," read one of their placards. "Join the Forest Workers Association," read a flyer, "and show your support for the Haida." And the non-Haida mayor of Port Clements, in the heart of logging country and himself a lifelong logger, said that "if we have to take sides, we're siding with the Haida. The long-term interests of the Haida Nation are more aligned with our interests than Weyerhaeuser's."

The mayor said he would really prefer the Haida, rather than Weyerhaeuser, to be his employer. In return, the Haida invited the Forest Workers Association and the International Woodworkers Association to convene at their next meeting on Haida Gwaii, where they were joined by Weyerhaeuser in agreeing to reduce the annual cut on the islands and respect the cultural, environmental, and economic values of the Haida Nation. A spokesman for Weyerhaeuser commented after the meeting that his company had been caught "in the middle of an epic battle between two sovereign powers." After siding for forty years with the Second Nation, they switched to the First. Here's how the current president of the Haida Nation saw it: "The truth is the Haida won the battle of Islands' Spirit Rising because almost everyone on the islands, Haida and non-Haida alike, actively supported the blockade."

Under the name BC Coalition for Sustainable Forest Solutions, no fewer than forty-nine NGOs representing labor unions,[23] churches, and environmental organizations openly supported the blockade, while a provincial poll indicated that three

23 A concurrent meeting of the BC Federation of Labor (which included the loggers' union) passed a resolution accusing the government of creating division between native and natural resource workers, and condemned the province for "cowardly use of the courts and police." "It wasn't the Indians who stopped the logging," read the communiqué. "It was the government." The president of the Fishermen's Union said this: "We as British Columbians should be glad that somebody has the guts to defy the law and say we're not going to allow the rape of our forests anymore." And this came from a Haida delegate from the Government and Service Employees' Union: "We will not become victims of cultural genocide. We are a nation forced into civil disobedience to protect the only future we have."

of five BC citizens wanted their province to negotiate native land claims. Moreover, the vast majority of people on the islands, including the non-Haida, supported Islands' Spirit Rising. However, only Haida were allowed on the blockade. This had to be seen as primarily *their* issue… a Haida issue, not an environmental issue.

Process servers turned up every morning with injunction papers, arriving just about the time the fire that warmed the protesters was getting low. The servers would be thanked for the fuel and asked if they had any more. Once again, the elders came to the barricades, some of them veterans of the Athlii Gwaii blockage of Lyell Island. A few were arrested, some of them in their nineties, one over one hundred years old. This time, they were sentenced to four to six months in jail by a judge who had ruled in an earlier case that aboriginal rights had been erased by colonial legislation. On appeal, no one served time, despite the fact that the judge who sentenced them predicted "the end of civilization" if the Haida got their way.

They did, and civilization survived, even though the annual timber cut on Haida Gwaii had been reduced from three million to eight hundred thousand cubic meters a year; several large areas of the archipelago had been set aside to protect culturally modified trees and the habitat of the endemic Queen Charlotte goshawk, the saw-whet owl, and the blue heron; and the annual bear hunt was ended forever (see sidebar on page 122). And for the first time in a century, the islands' timber quotas would not be set by the BC Forestry Department, but by the brand-new Haida Gwaii Management Council. Finally, aboriginal forest people, in at least one place on the planet, actually owned their trees.

While this was clearly another triumph for the Haida, not all of them were ready to declare victory. "It's not about winning," one elder observed. "It's about who we are becoming… We are helping the Crown restore its honor." With that sentiment in mind, the president of the Haida Nation wrote this letter to the governor general of Canada:

> Her Excellency the Right Honourable Adrienne Clarkson,
>
> We respectfully request your attention in the matter of the Honour of the Crown.[24]
>
> The history of the Haida Nation will show that for more than a century we have attempted to resolve the long-standing issues of Title dispute through diplomacy, negotiations, and appeals to your highest Court.
>
> Likewise, we have attempted to resolve the immediate issues of the use and exploitation of the resources of these lands vis-à-vis the Province of British Columbia.
>
> We have also worked diligently with our neighbors to design the conditions which would provide for the well-being of these islands as is necessary for a continuing culture and a sustainable economy.
>
> While Courts have made efforts to compel the Federal and Provincial Governments to sit down and resolve these matters through a fair process of reconciliation, British Columbia has responded with attempts to absolve itself of that responsibility.

24 The "Honour of the Crown" doctrine dates back to a notion that colonists brought with them called "the sacred trust of civilization." Part of the colonial paradigm, it was later replaced by a human rights paradigm reflected in various international declarations of human and indigenous rights, like the United Nations Declaration on the Rights of Indigenous Peoples, which are today more likely to be cited than "Honour of the Crown."

While we sought legal guidance through the Courts, British Columbia enacted legislation to divest itself of the legal authority and public duty to regulate the forests, and practically eliminated every public mechanism to oversee industrial and environmental accountability.

The Province has always put economic interests before the well-being of the land, and continues that pattern.

We note that the Supreme Court of Canada in its wisdom had opted for moral persuasion as the potential solution, and we agree, Honour should lead to the resolution of this dispute.

On the basis of the moral authority of your office and the sovereign responsibilities vested in you, we formally request your intervention in the delivery of the Honour of the Crown.

Respectfully,
Guujaaw,
President of the Haida Nation

The Annual Haida Gwaii Bear Hunt

BETWEEN 1983 and 2013, approximately 1,200 black bears were shot on Haida Gwaii by trophy hunters from around the world. The Haida had always opposed the annual hunt, appalled at the disrespect displayed in recreational killing under the authority of a provincial government. But British

The governor general of Canada is the official representative of the British monarch. When the king or queen of England truly ruled over the British Empire, and later the Commonwealth, of which Canada was one of fifteen member states, the governor general held a fairly powerful office. He (there were no women governor generals then) could actually veto legislation. Today, that isn't so, and although the governor general is constitutionally a "guarantor of continuous and stable governance and a nonpartisan safeguard against the abuse of power," his or her function is largely ceremonial. That said, an appearance or statement from any governor general is widely reported in the Canadian media. And their opinions are generally more respected than those of most politicians.

The governor general at the time the letter was written was Adrienne Clarkson, a refugee from Hong Kong who infused her office with new energy and eventually married Canadian philosopher John Ralston Saul. Both of them have been frequent visitors to Haida Gwaii and stalwart supporters of aboriginal rights in

Columbia, which had simply assumed sovereignty over the islands, ignored Haida demands to stop the mindless slaughter, and for thirty years issued licenses to kill the bears.

Most of the hunters were guided to the docile and fearless bears by two outfitters approved by the province. One permit was held by the owners of the Tlell River Lodge on Graham Island, the other by Pacific Bear Outfitters. Despite widespread public revulsion for trophy hunting, and research indicating growth opportunities in ecotourism activities such as viewing bears in their natural habitat, license owners continued to offer provincially approved "recreational bear hunting" (in other words, trophy hunting) tags.

No words were minced on licensee websites. Bear hunters traveling to Haida Gwaii, one site assured, "have a 100 percent opportunity with about 90 percent success at taking home a trophy bear."

"It's a world-class animal," another boasted. "You get a chance of killing a real exceptional old animal."

Pacific Bear Outfitters' fee for the first bear shot was $9,850 (an additional bear could be taken for $4,250). But the site stipulated that "trophy fees are paid on all animals shot—whether killed or wounded."

All the bears killed or wounded on Haida Gwaii were of a rare subspecies (*Ursus americanus carlottae*) found nowhere else in the world. They are also the largest black bears

Canada. So that letter, which was reprinted many times in many venues, was strategic and effective, even if the Right Honorable Ms. Clarkson took no action in direct response to it, which appears to be the case.

The Beginning
IN 2007, the Haida initiated their Strategic Land Use Agreement with the province that would more than double the area of land on the islands under protection and reduce the annual timber cut by half. But more precise targets had to be formulated for ecosystem-based management. In December, the agreement was signed and negotiation began with the province for full reconciliation.

Two years to the day later, on December 12, 2009, the Council of the Haida Nation signed a new land-use agreement with the province. Despite the fact that the agreement was signed almost forty years after the Haida's struggle with the government started, they called it the Kunst'aa Guu–Kunst'aayah Reconciliation Protocol (KKRP). (*Kunst'aa Guu* means "the beginning" in one of the two main dialects of Haida; *Kunst'aayah* means the same thing in the other dialect.) The name was carefully chosen to say that this move was only the beginning, the Haida believed, of a long reconciliation process, one that in many respects will still be under way long after this book is published.

The KKRP not only made another huge advance toward recognizing aboriginal title, but it also gave the Haida rightful stewardship over the entire Haida Nation—every island of the archipelago, or as they had claimed over and over again, "all that we say is ours." It also created the Haida Gwaii Management Council, comprised of two Haida and two provincial representatives and a jointly appointed chair (clearly modeled on the Archipelago Management Board that manages

on the planet. *Carlottae* is considered a "keystone species" on the islands because the bears transport salmon remains into surrounding forests of Haida Gwaii, where they fertilize the trees.

In 1995, the Council of the Haida Nation passed a resolution at its annual House of Assembly calling for an end to bear hunting on the islands, an activity which they described as "an unforgivable exercise in disrespect and disregard for the lives and spirits of creatures we hold to be our relations." The province ignored that until February 2004, when at a community land-planning forum cosponsored by the Haida Nation and the province, the President of the Haida Nation restated the Nation's position:

A just-completed economic study on grizzly bear hunting on the central coast shows that guides/outfitters could make more money viewing bears than they can shooting them. The Tlell River Lodge is in a good position to move from hunting to viewing. We ask you to please support the owners of the bear licenses on the islands in making a transition from recreational hunting to sustainable tourism.

Please join our initiative to protect the Haida Gwaii black bear by sharing your feelings on recreational bear hunting. Send an email from the list below asking the Tlell River Lodge to explore sustainable and locally supported activities.

Gwaii Haanas National Park). The council oversees and implements the Strategic Land Use Agreement of 2009, as well as all forest practices, the management of protected areas, and the protection of heritage sites. But most importantly, it determines the allowable forestry cut for Haida Gwaii, and that decision is legally binding. Compared to any previous land-use agreements or protocols signed between the government and First Nations in Canada, the KKRP is far more than a "beginning." It sets an inspiring standard for shared sovereignty that can be duplicated almost anywhere in the world. (Full text of the protocol is in appendix 5.)

Six months later, on June 17, 2010, the Haida invited the premier of British Columbia to visit their islands for a sacred ceremony. He agreed to come and arrived to find a large gathering of the most powerful and respected members of the Haida Nation, all dressed in full ceremonial garb.

They had invited him there, they said, to give him something…well, to give something back. It was the name Queen Charlotte Islands, which a British colony had bestowed upon the islands 150 years earlier. The name for the entire archipelago would once again be Haida Gwaii. And the Haida wanted the premier to know that they were not renaming the islands or "taking back a name." "We've always known this place to be Haida Gwaii. We're giving *you* back a name given to us by the Crown." Before the premier could express his gratitude and announce that all maps of the province would be amended to reflect the change, which he in fact did, the president of the Haida Nation added this: "What we are really doing here is unwinding colonialism." He continued:

> After a hundred years of conflict, we are setting the ground for a more productive era of peace. The interesting part is yet to come. How do we make this work? I think we can do it. And the world needs these little places to start turning the tide. I think we have a good chance to set an example.

Thousands of letters and signatures poured into the lodge and the province. On September 9, 2013, the British Columbia Ministry of Forests, Lands and Natural Resource Operations closed the black bear hunting season on Haida Gwaii forever.

The former Tlell River Hunting Lodge, now owned and operated by the Haida Nation and renamed Haida House, is the most popular ecotourism resort on the islands. The Haida did not regard their purchase of the lodge as a commercial venture.

"We're investing in life" was their stated motive.

EPILOGUE

"Idle No More"

Sovereignty cannot be separated from people or their culture.

Kirke Kickingbill

IN 1983, a special meeting on indigenous peoples was convened by the United Nations Human Rights Commission to explore ways that First Nations the world over could press the UN General Assembly for a recognition of their rights. Six years later, in 1989, seven hundred tribal Amazon leaders, convened by the Amazon-based Xavante and Kayapo, met in Altamira, Brazil. Some were from communities that had rarely been seen or contacted. In many ways, they were like the Haida had been two hundred years earlier. They were joined by environmentalists, biologists, progressive politicians, and media. It was the first time most of them had met, and the meeting drew worldwide attention to several big dams and other industrial developments planned for the Amazon region by the World Bank. And when Luis Macas, a delegate from La Confederación de Nacionalidades Indígenas del Ecuador, was quoted saying, "We are committed to peace, but if our needs are not met, we may have no option but armed struggle," national leaders in the Amazon region began taking their First Nations people more seriously. Not so long before, national armies, private militias, and death squads had been killing Indians in South America and Mesoamerica, few of whom ever fired back. But as Amazon governments became more progressive and accommodating of aboriginals, some even protecting native rights in their constitutions, an open war with them was not something any South American leader wanted, nor did the international community. That didn't stop all expressions of militancy in the indigenous community. The militancy just became less prone to violence and more to direct confrontation in national courts and capitols.

On May 28, 1990, about a thousand Quechua-speaking Indians took to the streets and occupied the Santo Domingo Church in Quito, Ecuador. "Five hundred years of residence" was their rallying cry. They sought restoration of indigenous homelands, compensation for environmental damages, and recognition of their language. In the mountains surrounding the city, trees were set on fire, haciendas occupied, and roads blockaded. Demonstrators were arrested and soldiers were taken hostage. The archbishop of Quito brokered a peace, but the action has kept the issues of aboriginal rights and title alive throughout the Amazon basin.

Three years later, the UN Assembly declared 1993 the "International Year of the World's Indigenous People." After the dedication, Erica-Irene Daes, chair of the UN Working Group on Indigenous Populations, suggested that the event was yet another example of tokenism and not the kind of recognition that was needed from the global community:

> It continues to be a matter of great disappointment to indigenous peoples, and to me, that some Member States cannot yet agree to include [us] in the family of nations. In an age which has overcome racism, racial discrimination and colonialism in so many fields, there are Member States that still perpetuate a myth as old as the European colonization of the Americas that indigenous peoples are legally unequal to other peoples.

The following year, the forty-eighth session of the UN General Assembly proclaimed the next ten years to be the "International Decade of the World's Indigenous Peoples," established a working group of the Human Rights Commission for the cause, and began the long, drawn-out process of drafting the Declaration on the Rights of Indigenous Peoples.

The UN Permanent Forum on Indigenous Issues was established in 2000 and began to gather every year, yet received little attention or support from member nations. Ted Moses, ambassador from the Grand Council of the Crees in Quebec, described the forum as "an orphan within the UN system... barely recognized or acknowledged." He lamented, "It appears not to affect the work of the United Nations."

While the drafting and approval of the Declaration on the Rights of Indigenous Peoples dragged on, indigenous peoples

formed new "pockets of resistance" and pressed other international bodies such as the Inter-American Court of Human
Rights, the International Labor Organization, the Convention on
Biological Diversity, the World Council on Indigenous Peoples,
the Organization of American States, and the African Union, all
of which have passed international instruments supporting indigenous peoples' rights to the following:

- Self-determination
- Ownership control and use of communal lands
- Free disposition of their natural wealth and resources
- No deprivation of their means of subsistence
- Free enjoyment of their own culture and traditional
  way of life
- Informed consent prior to activities on their lands
- Self-representation through their own institutions
- Free exercise of customary laws
- Restitution of and compensation for land already lost

Although many of these instruments are not fully enforceable,[25] despite their inclusion in treaties and frequent citation in
litigation, they are often regarded as a body of international law
protecting indigenous rights, and both the powerful International
Union for the Conservation of Nature and its World Commission
on Protected Areas have recognized these advances and called
upon governments to comply with them. But as long as the declarations behind international law remained largely unenforceable,

25 The International Labor Organization's Convention 169 legally binds all states that formally ratified it. However,
not all indigenous peoples like it, some saying it's a Eurocentric, assimilationist document that ignores indigenous
worldviews and gives mere "lip service" to aboriginal law and legal systems. But many do support its adoption,
including the Sami, the Inuit, and the World Council on Indigenous Peoples.

the only way for aboriginal societies to regain true sovereignty was to go mano a mano with the nation-state, province, or Crown that enveloped them after "discovery."

* * *

FINALLY, AFTER more than two decades of heated international debate, on September 13, 2007, the United Nations General Assembly got around to voting on the Declaration on the Rights of Indigenous Peoples (UNDRIP). One hundred and forty-three nations were in favor, eleven abstained, and four (Australia, New Zealand, Canada, and the United States) voted against the measure. All four have subsequently withdrawn their opposition, but in each case emphasizing that they regard the declaration as "aspirational" and nonbinding, which to indigenous leaders is simply another subtle form of nullification.

When Canada reversed its position on the declaration, it described it as a document "which speaks to the individual and collective rights of Indigenous peoples… [but] does not reflect customary international law nor change Canadian laws." That contradicts previous statements and positions taken by the Supreme Court and previous administrations of Canada. To say the declaration is merely "aspirational" defies both Canadian and international law.

The generic message of aspirational voters might sound something like this: Yes, we approve of UNDRIP as something indigenous peoples should aspire to, but if they go too far toward demanding title and independence, we will fight them every step of the way.

The only country so far to fully ratify UNDRIP and implement it as domestic law is Bolivia, where over half the national population (including the current president) is aboriginal. Most of the countries who either did not sign the declaration or expressed reservations about it expressed concern about the vague definition of *self-determination*, despite the fact that article 46, paragraph 1, clearly states that it does not offer indigenous peoples a right to secede or create their own state.

Although under article 12 of the UN Charter, a declaration is nonbinding, it is also "a solemn instrument" deserving of utmost respect "where maximum compliance is expected." So when UNDRIP affirms that "indigenous peoples are equal to all other peoples," it's making a strong statement that articulates the individual and collective rights of 370 million First Nation citizens, as well as endorsing the self-determination of their culture, identity, language, and political status, while emphasizing their right to remain distinct, pursue their own visions of social development, maintain and strengthen their own institutions and traditions, and pursue the economic system of their choice without assimilating into the larger society.

The declaration also prohibits international discrimination against indigenous peoples and advocates their full participation in all matters concerning them. It also guarantees their right to participate, if they choose to, in the political, economic, social, and cultural life of the state or states that annexed or enveloped their homeland.

The text of the declaration includes a few things that read a lot like sections of the Haida Constitution:

- Article 4 guarantees "autonomy, or self-government in matters relating to internal and local affairs."
- Article 8 protects indigenous peoples from "dispossession of their lands, territories or resources."
- Article 10 reads, "Indigenous peoples shall not be forcibly removed from their lands or territories. No relocation shall take place without the free, prior and informed consent of the indigenous peoples concerned and after agreement on just and fair compensation and, where possible, with the option of return."
- Article 18 reads, "Indigenous peoples have the right to participate in decision-making in matters which would affect their rights, through representatives chosen by themselves in accordance with their own procedures, as well as to maintain and develop their own indigenous decision-making institutions."
- Article 19 reads, "States shall consult and cooperate in good faith with the indigenous peoples concerned through their own representative institutions in order to obtain their free, prior and informed consent before adopting and implementing legislative or administrative measures that may affect them."
- And perhaps most significant to the Haida's forty-year struggle for sovereignty, article 26 states, "1. Indigenous peoples have the right to the lands, territories and resources which they have traditionally owned, occupied or otherwise used or acquired. 2. Indigenous peoples have the right to own, use, develop and control the lands, territories and resources that they possess by reason of

traditional ownership or other traditional occupation or use, as well as those which they have otherwise acquired. 3. States shall give legal recognition and protection to these lands, territories and resources. Such recognition shall be conducted with due respect to the customs, traditions and land tenure systems of the indigenous peoples concerned."

If they could really be enforced, or moved from the vague canons of international law to real domestic statute, those articles would protect native homelands like Haida Gwaii and their inhabitants from being marginalized in future negotiations between them and national governments. And each article could be cited by native communities in any UN member nation as a binding declaration in support of their sovereignty. In fact, in countries that accept customary international law, *opinio juris*,[26] as part of their domestic law, indigenous peoples would benefit from the authoritative International Law Association's Resolution No. 5/2012 on the Rights of Indigenous Peoples, which without any opposition, found that indigenous peoples' rights to their traditional lands, culture, and internal self-government was guaranteed by international law.

Unfortunately, as I said earlier, international law in countries such as Canada might not be fully enforceable, nor are UN declarations legally binding, even to signatory states. They do, however, represent the dynamic development of international legal norms and reflect the commitment of signatory states to move in the right direction, and abide by the basic principles of human

26 The sense of legal obligation. In international law, acceptance of a practice as sufficient to create legal obligations.

rights. This is the case for UNDRIP, which, despite matters of enforceability, is still expected to have a major effect on the rights of indigenous peoples worldwide, simply by establishing important standards for their treatment and providing a significant tool toward eliminating human rights violations and combating discrimination and marginalization against over 370 million people.

General Assembly President Sheikha Haya Rashed Al Kalifa described the declaration's passage as another "major step toward the promise and protection of human rights and fundamental freedom for all." However, she warned that "even with this progress, indigenous people still face marginalization, extreme poverty and other human rights violations." And she predicts that they would still be "dragged into conflicts and land disputes that threaten their way of life and very survival."

San Bushman Jumanda Gakelebone called from the office of First People of the Kalahari in Botswana to say how "happy and thrilled" he was "to hear about the adoption of this declaration, which," he says, "recognizes that governments can no longer treat us as second-class citizens and throw us off our lands like they did." And Kenyan Ogiek leader Peter Kiplangat Cheruiot believes that if signatories abide by the declaration, it will place "the lives of [millions of] indigenous peoples on an equal footing with the rest of the world's citizens."

New Zealand's Waitangi Tribunal, established by a treaty between the government and the Maori, concluded that the declaration "represents the most important statement of indigenous rights ever formulated." And in 2011, the Australian Human Rights Commission recommended that "all legislation, policies and programs [in Australia] be reviewed for consistency with the rights affirmed by the Declaration." And the government of Norway stated that "the Declaration contextualizes all existing human rights for indigenous peoples and provides therefore the natural frame of reference for work and debate relating to the promotion of indigenous peoples' rights."

UNDRIP was a long time coming. It reflects decades of perseverance and hard work by people who had already formed a thousand or more "pockets of resistance" and declared themselves "idle no more." It was a triumphant accomplishment, and in the history of this remarkable social movement will long be remembered by native people the world over, as will the date: September 13, 2007, a day that will also be quietly celebrated by the elders of Haida Gwaii.

* * *

WHILE THE legal foundations of imperial domination are arbitrary and dubious, they have survived as long as they have because they were supported and affirmed by courts created by imperial states. National and provincial courts were not created to interpret international or aboriginal law. They are there to interpret the laws and constitutions of the nations that created them. So if the land and property rights of that nation remain based, even to a degree, on doctrines like terra nullius or fee-simple land ownership established and protected by the Discovery Doctrine, they are not likely to be supportive of aboriginal title or rights.

However, just because international law has been a friend of colonialism doesn't mean it can't now become a friend of the colonized, as it already has in the many ways mentioned above. The good news is that today not a single nation-state in the world formally opposes UNDRIP, a fact that clearly enhances its legal status and impact.

I asked Siegfried Wiessner, a prominent professor of international law at Saint Thomas University in Miami who has studied and written extensively about international law and indigenous sovereignty, to read this chapter for legal and historical accuracy. He did so and offered this response:

> Indigenous sovereignty, like any claim to sovereignty, is not granted. It inheres in its bearer; it grows, or it dies, from within. The UN Declaration on the Rights of Indigenous Peoples is based on the universal recognition of their claim to self-determination on their lands, an aspiration that lies at the heart of the rising indigenous peoples' claims to re-empowerment.
>
> The declaration reaffirms preexisting rules of customary international law and treaty law. The right to recapture identity, to reinvigorate ways of life, to reconnect with the earth, to regain traditional lands, to protect heritage, to revitalize languages and manifest culture—all of these rights are as important to indigenous people as the right to make final decisions in their internal political, judicial, and economic settings.
>
> The flame of self-determination, however, needs to burn from inside the community itself. International and domestic law can and should stand ready to kindle, protect, and grow this flame until it burns fiercely, illuminating the path for the ultimate goal of self-realization of indigenous peoples around the world.

The flame of self-determination has never ceased burning on Haida Gwaii, and doubtless it never will, as a new generation of well-educated Haida youth rise to leadership, determined to keep and protect "all that we say is ours." And they heed the advice of Guujaaw, former president of the Haida Nation, who reminds them often that "Drawing the line is the easy part, holding the line is the challenge."

APPENDICES

APPENDIX 1:

Haida Timeline

1901 — Logging began on Haida Gwaii.

1924 — *The Allied Tribes of BC* and *Native Brotherhood* were formed.

1973 — *Calder.* The Supreme Court ruled that the Nisga'a did hold title to their traditional lands before British Columbia was created. The Court split evenly on whether Nisga'a still had title. The federal government adopted a comprehensive land-claims policy. BC refused to participate.

For the first time, the Court decided that aboriginal title is a legal right to land that does not depend on the Royal Proclamation of 1763. However, the Court split evenly on whether Aaboriginal title had been legislatively extinguished in British Columbia prior to the province joining Canada in 1871.

The *Calder* decision caused the federal government to reassess the policy of refusing to recognize aboriginal land rights that it had generally followed since the late 1920s. Soon after that court decision, it created the comprehensive land-claims policy to deal with aboriginal title claims, and participated in the James Bay and Northern Quebec Agreement (1975), the first modern-day treaty to be negotiated. It also set up a specific claims process to deal with past violations of treaty rights, unlawful taking of reserve lands, and other matters.

When patriation of the Canadian Constitution and inclusion of the Charter of Rights and Freedoms came to dominate the political agenda in the late 1970s, aboriginal leaders lobbied for constitutional recognition of aboriginal and treaty rights. This was accomplished by the inclusion of section 35(1) in the Constitution Act of 1982, which reads: "The existing aboriginal and treaty rights of the aboriginal peoples of Canada are hereby recognized and affirmed." Section 35(2) defines the aboriginal peoples of Canada as including the "Indian, Inuit and Métis peoples."

Section 35 is a landmark in acknowledgment of the rights of the aboriginal peoples. It has largely determined the political and legal discourse on aboriginal rights since 1982.

1974 — The Council of the Haida Nation formed and decided to pursue a land claim.

A petition calling for a Moresby logging moratorium received five hundred signatures.

ITT-Rayonier presented a five-year logging plan to the Ministry of Forests that proposed moving the Frank Beban logging operation from Talunkwen Island to Burnaby Island.

The Islands Protection Society (IPS) was formed: Haida and newcomers joined together to seek protection of wilderness areas on Moresby Island.

IPS met with Skidegate Band Council. The councils objected to the logging plan due to Haida reliance on the area.

Premier Dave Barrett made a verbal commitment to the Skidegate Band to impose a logging moratorium on traditional food-gathering areas in TFL 24, but this action meant only a deferral of logging in small areas of Gwaii Haanas.

1975 — Logging began on Lyell Island.

1976 — Haida Museum opened in Skidegate.

1978 — ITT- Rayonier's tree farm licence expired.

Chief T'aanuu (Nathan Young) and Guujaaw with IPS took Rayonier and the minister of forests to court in an attempt to stop logging. Chief T'aanuu and Guujaaw obtained standing in the court; IPS was denied it. The court action was a "judicial review" to stop renewal of the TFL. The deputy minister of forests advised the court that the province was quite willing to meet with the Haida to alleviate their concerns. The petition was denied by the Supreme Court of BC because the minister of forests had not made a decision and the license had not yet been renewed. The court encouraged that the meeting with the deputy minister proceed before the renewal.

Haida citizens began watching southern village sites on a volunteer basis.

1979 — *Haida v. BC* re TFL 24.

A South Moresby Planning Team was created to study the issues over logging in South Moresby. Logging continued on Lyell Island while the planning team worked on a report.

1980 — Haida's formal land claim to Ottawa was declined.

1981 — Haida elected Grand Chief Percy Williams.

Haida announces registration of formal land claim with federal government.

The CHN designated Duu Guusd Tribal Park, on the west coast, and petitioned the province to defer all development plans within the Tribal Park.

1982 — The United Fisherman and Allied Workers' Union and Native Brotherhood, the two main fishing organizations on the coast, recognized Duu Guusd Tribal Park and supported the designation, as did the Graham Island Advisory Planning Commission.

Haida people rejected the terms of reference of an Islands task force study on a county system of local government proposed by the BC government, but then persuaded task force members to join them in exploring other forms of local government.

The Constitution Act's section 35 entrenched aboriginal and treaty rights.

1983 — A feast was held at Naden Harbour to declare Duu Guusd.

The first All-Islands Symposium was organized. Haida sent emissary Don Rosenbloom to Japan to request owners of CIPA Industries Ltd., the logging company in Duu Guusd, to cease operations.

1984 — The South Moresby Planning Team delivered its report to the provincial cabinet's Environment and Land Use Committee (ELUC). BC sat on the report and logging continued.

The Council of the Haida Nation held a series of meetings with government ministers offering to develop a solution.

Islands on the Edge was published.

1985 — Gwaii Haanas was declared a heritage site. The Watchmen program began.

The Haida people and other Islands residents staged a logging blockade of Lyell Island.

CIPA Industries Ltd. dissolved. The provincial government passed up the chance to cancel cutting rights in Duu Guusd.

CHN met with minister of parks, Tony Brummet, who stated that no cutting permits would be issued while the Haida Nation and BC were talking or before a formal decision was made on the whole of South Moresby.

Logging on Lyell Island slowed down as the logging quota had been cut and Frank Beban's contract with Western Forest Products was due to expire.

The minister of forests announced that logging would continue on remaining portions of Lyell Island, excluding Windy Bay.

Haida met with the minister of environment, Austin Pelton, who agreed that logging must cease after forty days. If it did not stop, the Haida Nation would consider it an act of aggression.

Haida met with ELUC, who assured them that no further timber-cutting permits would be issued until a formal decision on land allocation for South Moresby was announced.

The minister of forests issued three new permits in an area on the south side of Lyell Island. These new permits exceeded Frank Beban's annual cut quota in volume.

The minister of environment, Pelton, announced a Wilderness Advisory Committee that would study South Moresby and the Duu Guusd Tribal Park, among other areas.

Logging resumed on Lyell Island in October. The Haida Nation moved to set up a camp at Sedgewick Bay. Twenty-five RCMP officers were stationed at the Beban logging camp.

The camp moved from Sedgewick Bay to Windy Bay. The Haida Nation blocked the road on Lyell Island.

Western Forest Products filed for and was granted an injunction. The Haida went back to the blockade but, on the first day, stood aside to let the loggers pass in respect of the courts.

On November 16, Haida elders were arrested at Lyell Island. The blockade and arrests continued through November. Beban applied for contempt charges against seventeen Haidas.

BC's attorney general announced that he would intervene in the public interest and introduce more severe charges for the arrested Haida.

Frank Beban and crew approached the line.

BC Supreme Court authorized serving of contempt of court and mischief charges against seventeen Haidas.

Ten of the seventeen had their charges of contempt upheld and were sentenced to five-month suspended sentences and denied access to Lyell Island.

CHN designated Gwaii Haanas land and marine areas as a Haida Heritage Site.

Information came forward showing that the majority of the provincial cabinet, including the Premier, were shareholders in Western Forest Products, the company that was doing the logging.

Skeena Member for Parliament Jim Fulton raised the issue of aboriginal rights and title and the events unfolding on Lyell Island in the House of Commons. The issues were debated in the Commons.

The Constitution of Haida Nation was revised.

Ten Haida (including Guuj) were convicted of contempt.

1986 — Of the seventy-two Haida charged, eleven had their charges changed to a criminal breach of a court order. The others had a stay of proceedings. One of the eleven had charges dropped at a later date.

Eight appeared before a judge and elected to represent themselves.

A salmon stream was wiped out by a logging-induced slide. Frank Beban was charged with an offense under the Fisheries Act and ordered to appear.

In March, the Western Canada Wilderness Committee's Save South Moresby caravan set out. Beginning in Saint John's, Newfoundland, the caravan traveled 7,500 kilometers across Canada. The tour rallied support for the protection of South Morseby through a series of whistle-stops. Fund-raising and benefit concerts with the likes of Long John Baldry, Pete Seeger, and Bruce Cockburn occured and further raised awareness. Elders Ada Yovanovich, Ethel Jones, Gaahlaay, and Watson Pryce joined the train along the way.

Haida built a longhouse at Windy Bay.

Loo Taas paddled six hundred miles from Vancouver and arrived home. That evening at a feast in Skidegate, the minister of environment, Tom McMillan, announced that the federal and provincial governments would designate South Moresby as a national park reserve.

The Gowgaia Foundation (Earthlife Canada Foundation) was established to promote sustainability on Haida Gwaii.

Miles and Gujj renounced their Canadian citizenship.

1987 — Canada and BC signed MOU on Gwaii Haanas.

1988 — The South Moresby Agreement signed between the federal and provincial governments designated Gwaii Haanas as a national park reserve, pending the settlement of aboriginal rights and title over the same area designated by the Council of the Haida Nation. As a part of this agreement, the federal government put up $106 million, most of which went to pay off the logging companies, contractors, and loggers. A $36 million "community development fund" to stimulate the economy came to the islands.

Representatives of the Council of the Haida Nation advised the government of Canada that there would be no spending of the community development fund until there was an agreement between the government of Canada and the Haida Nation.

The CHN and communities came to an agreement. Rather than spending the $36 million fund over eight years as was proposed, the money would become a perpetual fund and only the interest would be spent.

1989 — Haida passports were issued. The Ministry of Aboriginal Affairs was formed.

1990 — *Sparrow* confirmed aboriginal rights existing in 1982. The Musqueam people's aboriginal right to fish for food and ceremonial purposes was not extinguished.

British Columbia agreed to join the First Nations and Canada in treaty negotiations.

First Nations, BC, and Canada agreed to establish a task force (*BC Claims Task Force*) to develop a process for land-claim negotiations in BC. In June, the task force issued nineteen recommendations.

1991 — Chief Justice McEachern dismissed the Gitxsan-Wet'suwet'en chiefs' claim in the case of *Delgamuukw v. Her Majesty the Queen*.

Nisga'a Tribal Council, BC, and Canada signed a tripartite framework agreement that set out the scope, process, and topics for negotiations. The agreement was reached outside of the usual treaty process.

In spite of provincial legislative issues and other encumbrances, and after years of hearing why the community agreement wouldn't work, the Gwaii Trust Interim Planning Society (GTIPS) was formed. GTIPS's purpose was to develop a permanent model for a locally controlled, interest-generating fund.

The K'iis Gwaii action saw the Haida Nation take a stand on the sports fishing lodges moving into Haida Gwaii.

Twelve people were charged over K'iis Gwaii and seven were convicted of criminal contempt of a Supreme Court of BC. The conviction went to the BC Court of Appeal and was overturned, resulting in no criminal records.

1992 — The Forest Stewardship Council was founded, and market campaigns began in Europe to boycott timber cut in old-growth forests.

The First Nations Summit, Canada, and BC established the Treaty Commission.

1993 — The BC Treaty Commission began the treaty negotiation process.

CHN and Canada signed the Gwaii Haanas Agreement, which sets out the government-to-government and management relationship for Gwaii Haanas, with a commitment to include the marine area at a future date. The joint agreement was the first of its kind and was accomplished without compromising Haida rights and title.

Both governments commited to cooperatively manage the Gwaii Haanas terrestrial area and to work toward an agreement for the adjacent marine area.

The Gwaii Haanas Archipelago Management Board was established. Two Haida and two Gwaii Haanas representatives were appointed to the AMB.

Gwaii Haanas took on the Haida Gwaii Watchmen program.

1994 — The BC Treaty Commission, BC, and Canada held initial meetings with the forty-two First Nations who had submitted statements of intent to negotiate. The Gwaii Trust Society was formed to operate the perpetual trust fund, and GTIPS was dissolved. The Gwaii Trust Society's vision was to support an Islands community characterized by respect for cultural diversity, the environment, and a sustainable and increasingly self-sufficient economy. The Forest Practices Code was introduced and enacted.

1995 — *CHN v. Forestry and MacBlo.*
The Haida claim for aboriginal title was dismissed.

1996 — The Nisga'a, BC, and Canada signed an Agreement-In-Principle.
The Royal Commission on Aboriginal Peoples released its monumental Report, the most in-depth study of aboriginal issues ever undertaken. But while the Report was cited several times by the Supreme Court, it did not appear to have much of an impact on government policy.
The Islands Community Stability Initiative released the Consensus Document.

1997 — The Supreme Court of BC handed down its unanimous decision on the *Delgamuukw* case. The Court ruled that aboriginal title to the land had never been extinguished. The previous trial judge had erred by not accepting oral history as evidence in the case. The claim was sent back to trial, suggesting that negotiations were the best way to resolve outstanding claims. Rules that lands held pursuant to aboriginal title cannot be used in a manner that is irreconcilable with the nature of the attachment to the land which forms the basis of the group's claim to aboriginal title. This decision was widely regarded as a turning point for treaty negotiations in BC and confirmed existence of aboriginal title.
Oil and gas rights were relinquished within the proposed Gwaii Haanas Marine Conservation Reserve. The Supreme Court of Canada handed down the *Delgamuukw* decision.
The CEO of MacMillan Bloedel commissioned a comprehensive review of the company's forest policies in coastal BC

operations. The review concluded that traditional clear-cutting approaches to forest management were no longer meeting public expectations.

1998 — The Haida Accord was signed by the CHN, Hereditary Leaders, Old Massett Village Council, and Skidegate Band Council.

Community Futures was established through the Gwaii Trust and Western Diversification to support community-led economic development.

Operation Herring Storm swung into action to protect herring stocks on Haida Gwaii.

1999 — The First Nations' Summit gave support to CHN Title Case.

Guujaw became president of the Haida Nation.

2000 — The CHN launched the TFL 39 Case in the Supreme Court of British Columbia.

The Nisga'a Treaty became law.

Thirteen First Nations, including the Haida, met and signed the Turning Point Declaration.

Halfyard dismissed *CHN v. BC & Weyerhauser.*

2001 — Haida Nation filed Title and Rights case in BC Court. The BC Court of Appeal upheld the TFL 39 judgment requiring the province and industry to consult and accommodate the Haida Nation.

The Haida House of Assembly ratified the Haida Constitution.

The CHN and the province agreed to a co-chaired land-use planning process guided by ecosystem based management (EBM) and a government-to-government negotiation to address unresolved matters between the parties.

The Assembly approved a one-thousand-year plan for cedar.

2002 — Ninety percent of the on-island Weyerhaeuser employees formed an association to fight status quo forest policies.

BC Court of Appeals overturned Halfyard.

CHN writ in BC Supreme Court.

Haida statement of claim was filed.

2003 — The Province "offered" 20 percent of Haida Gwaii land base to the Haida Nation in return for shelving the title case and "restarting treaty negotiations." This offer was characterized by the CHN as "posturing" and "mischief," and they wondered, "Why should we give up 80 percent of our land?"

The Haida Gwaii/Queen Charlotte Islands Land Use Planning process began. Planning started with the Community Planning Forum, co-chaired by BC and the CHN with the Haida Land Use Vision as the guiding document.

The Heritage Tourism Association spent two years developing an Island vision strategy that was not implemented.

An All-Islands Symposium was held to discuss successes, explore commonalities, and learn from each other.

A Unity Feast was held in Queen Charlotte that evening to celebrate the common vision among Island residents.

New government policies saw more export of raw logs and the floating of provincial government responsibilities to industry.

Island residents announced the Island's Spirit Rising movement and established "checkpoints" at the Yakoun River and Queen Charlotte.

A Memorandum of Understanding was signed with the province of BC, which became the basis for Reconciliation of Title negotiations.

National Geographic Traveler magazine rated Gwaii Haanas as number one on its Destination Scorecard.

2004 — Haida Land Use Vision (HLUV) was presented at the Land Use Table in February.

The Forest and Range Practices Act (FRPA) was introduced, which was a new results-based code that was less prescriptive and put more reliance on professional judgment of foresters and other forest professionals.

Statistics were published: for the years 1900 to 2004, 102 million cubic meters of wood had been logged over an area of 168,000 hectares on Haida Gwaii.

Canada Supreme Court ruled that BC has duty to consult.

2005 — The Islands' Spirit Rising blockade took place.
Weyerhauser TFL sale to Brascan.

In February, the land-use planning process ended and recommendations of the Community Planning Forum were made to the BC government and the CHN to begin government-to-government negotiation on the Strategic Land Use Agreement (SLUA). A consensus for a recommendation wasn't reached.

In *Haida Nation v. BC Minister of Forests*, the Supreme Court of Canada concluded that the province had failed to meet its duties to consult and accommodate in respect of the transfer of control and replacement of TFL 39. This decision set out the nature and scope of obligations to consult and accommodate for the first time.

The Forest Range and Evaluation Program (FREP) was introduced, with the purpose of evaluating whether practices under FRPA were meeting the intent of objectives and sustainable use of resources.

The Haida people and other Haida Gwaii residents held Islands' Spirit Rising, a protest due to the transfer of TFL 39 from Weyerhaeuser to Cascadia without adequate consultation.

On May 11, a Letter of Understanding on the new approach to land-use planning was signed by the BC government and the CHN as a result of negotiations to end the blockade.

The provincial government committed to develop a Strategic Land Use Plan (SLUP) and provide the Haida with a 120,000-cubic-meter tenure plus about $5 million in revenue sharing.

2006 — The Village of Queen Charlotte signed the Protocol Agreement.

The Community Viability Strategy Steering Committee, consisting of band, local, and regional government officials and chaired by the BC government and the CHN, worked on the future economic development of Haida Gwaii.

2007 — The Declaration on the Rights of Indigenous Peoples (UNDRIP) is voted on.

The Haida Nation and the province of BC signed a draft Haida Gwaii Strategic Land Use Agreement. The plan protected about 50 percent of Haida Gwaii, and the remaining land base was subjected to ecosystem-based management.

The Gwaii Forest Society was formed to receive $24 million from the South Moresby Forest Replacement Account.

Gwaii Haanas's management arrangement and quota system was challenged in court by Moresby Explorers Ltd. The court ruled that the management and quota system was legal and an innovative solution; upon appeal, the case was dismissed.

Roger Williams decision addressing aboriginal rights of the Tsilhqot'in people in the interior of BC. The court concluded the Tsilhqot'in had an aboriginal right to hunt and trap throughout the claim area, but the court was unable to make a declaration on aboriginal title because of a technicality of the proceedings.

On December 12, Guujaaw, president of the Council of the Haida Nation, and BC Premier Gordon Campbell signed the Haida Gwaii Strategic Land Use Agreement (SLUA).

2008 — Sandspit signed the Protocol Agreement. A new sign was placed at the Ministry of Forests that read "Haida Gwaii Forest District."

In August, the Haida Heritage Centre at Kaay Linagaay had its grand opening. The Centre also incorporated and expanded the Haida Gwaii Museum in Skidegate on the centuries-old Haida Qay'llnagaay village site.

Depression occured in forest industry and overall economy (more severe than the cyclical downturns of 1997, 2000, 2004–5).

The Misty Islands Economic Development Society was formed with $500,000 funding from the BC government.

Haida vowed to return the Queen Charlotte Islands' name to the Crown.

2009 — The Kunst'aa Guu–Kunst'aayah Reconciliation Protocol was signed with the province of BC. The protocol outlined a process to reconcile Haida and Crown titles.

Gaaysiigang, an ocean forum for Haida Gwaii, was held at Kay Llnagaay. Western Forest Products on indefinite shutdown/ layoff (TFL 6).

In February, the BC government and the CHN agreed on an 800,000-cubic-meter annual allowable cut under the SLUA.

The Integrated Land Management Bureau projected SLUA implementation to be completed by December (i.e., legal objectives), and approved by the cabinet and brought into force by January 2010.

2010 — The Gwaii Haanas Marine Agreement was signed by the CHN and Canada in January. The agreement put in place a cooperative management partnership to protect and conserve the marine ecosystem of the proposed national marine conservation area reserve and confirmed the boundaries of the marine area.

The Gwaii Haanas National Marine Conservation Area Reserve and Haida Heritage Site was formally established.

Giving the Name Back with Respect Ceremony took place in Old Massett. The name Queen Charlotte Islands was given back to the province of BC, and provincial maps would be changed, identifying the islands as Haida Gwaii.

The twenty-fifth anniversary of Athlii Gwaii.

APPENDIX 2:

Strategic Land Use Agreement

HAIDA GWAII
STRATEGIC LAND USE AGREEMENT

BETWEEN

The Indigenous People of Haida Gwaii
as represented by
The Council of the Haida Nation
(the "Haida")

AND

The Province of British Columbia
(the "Province")

as represented by
The Minister of Agriculture and Lands

(Each a "Party" and collectively the "Parties")

September 13, 2007

WHEREAS:

a) A community-based, strategic land use planning process, involving a community planning forum and jointly chaired by the Parties, was initiated for the Haida Gwaii (Queen Charlotte Islands) in September of 2003;

b) The planning process was based on two protocol agreements signed in April of 2001, in which the Province and the Haida committed to: i) cooperative development of a strategic land use plan, guided by an ecosystem based management (EBM) framework; and ii) a government-to-government process for attempted resolution of the outstanding matters agreed upon by the Parties;

c) The planning process ended in February 2005 and the recommendations of the community planning forum were forwarded to the Parties for further consideration;

d) The Parties signed a May 11, 2005 Letter of Understanding that included a commitment to develop and implement a "new approach to land use planning," building on the previous work already done in the land use planning process (including discussions related to EBM), maintaining the interests of the island community, connecting land and resources to community viability, and reaching completion in a timely manner;

e) The Parties initialled a Draft Agreement on May 29, 2007 for discussion and have since agreed to make changes that are set out in this Land Use Agreement;

f) The Parties are committed to fostering a respectful and coordinated working relationship on Haida Gwaii;

g) The Parties acknowledge that they are engaged in other discussions that are expected to result in new arrangements for land and resource decision-making and management.

THE PARTIES AGREE AS FOLLOWS:

1.0   Definitions

In this Agreement and any Attachments:

A. **"Detailed Strategic Plan"** or **"Detailed Strategic Planning"** means a plan or planning process, respectively, that is jointly developed by the Parties pursuant to this Land Use Agreement for landscapes, watersheds and other areas with content that is consistent with ecosystem based management objectives, including stream restoration objectives;

B. **"EBM Objectives"** means the management objectives set out in Attachment B;

C. **"Ecosystem Based Management"** (herein "EBM") on Haida Gwaii means an adaptive, systematic approach to managing human activities, that seeks to ensure the co-existence of healthy, fully functioning ecosystems and human communities;

D. **"Land Use Zone"** means an area of land as shown and described in Attachment A that has assigned values, uses and management provisions that are distinct from adjacent areas;

E. **"Land Use Agreement"** means this Strategic Land Use Agreement, and any future amendments subsequently agreed upon by the Parties;

F. **"Operating Area"** means the Operating Area, as shown on Attachment A, identified for continued resource development and management activities, including forest harvesting and forest management in accordance with ecosystem based management objectives;

G. **"Special Value Area"** means the Special Value Area, as shown on Attachment A, identified as 100% (percent) forest retention for critical nesting habitat for goshawk, great blue heron, and saw-whet owl; and

H. **"New Protected Area"** means the New Protected Area, as shown on Attachment A, identified for ecological and cultural conservation, spiritual and recreational purposes.

2.0   Purpose

2.1   This Land Use Agreement is intended to address the outcomes of the Haida Gwaii land use planning process recommendations, and to amend and finalize the draft government-to-government Agreement initialed by the Parties on May 29, 2007 respecting strategic land use on Haida Gwaii.

2.2   This Land Use Agreement is intended to confirm strategic land use zones and EBM Objectives and provide a framework for its collaborative implementation by the Parties, including:

   a) The use of interim and permanent protection measures;

   b) The analysis, testing, subsequent verification, and establishment of land use objectives implementing EBM; and

   c) The establishment of appropriate management structures, including structures to oversee the implementation of EBM on Haida Gwaii.

3.0   Parts of this Land Use Agreement

3.1   This Land Use Agreement includes sections 1.0 to 10.0 and the following attachments:

   a) Attachment A – Land Use Zones and Attributes;

   b) Attachment B – EBM Management Objectives;

   c) Attachment C – Map of Monumental, Archaeological and Cultural Cedar

Forest Resource Value Areas;

d) Attachment D – Map of Marbled Murrelet Nesting Habitat Areas;

e) Attachment E – Structures for Implementing the Agreement.

3.2 The attachments to this Land Use Agreement are an integral part of this Agreement, as if set out at length in the body of this Land Use Agreement.

4.0   Land Use Zones

4.1 The Parties agree to the New Protected Areas, Operating Areas, and Special Value Areas as shown on Attachment A.

4.2 The Haida have designated the New Protected Areas and Special Value Areas as Haida Natural, Cultural and Spiritual Areas, and will maintain these areas in accordance with their laws, policies, customs, traditions and decision making processes.

4.3 Upon signing this Land Use Agreement, Provincial representatives will initiate the following actions for the New Protected Areas and Special Value Areas shown in Attachment A:

a) Establish (where none exist) and continue Part 13 designations under the *Forest Act*, for a period of two years from the date of signing of the Agreement;

b) Establish (where none exist) and continue "no registration reserves" under the *Mineral Tenure Act*, "no disposition reserves" under the *Coal Act*, and notices for "no disposition" under the *Petroleum and Natural Gas Act* and *Geothermal Resources Act*, for a period of two years from the date of signing of the Agreement;

c) Establish (where none exist) and continue "withdrawals from disposition" under the *Land Act*, for a period of two years from the date of signing of the Agreement; and

d) The use of Detailed Strategic Planning to determine more precise locations and final designations for the Special Value Areas, including:

i) Wildlife Habitat Areas and General Wildlife Measures in accordance with *Forest and Range Practices Act*;

ii) Old Growth Management Areas in accordance with *Land Use Objectives Regulation*;

iii) Traditional forest resources/features in accordance with *Land Use Objectives Regulations* or the *Forest and Range Practices Act*; and

iv) Other management area designations available to address critical habitat for threatened or endangered species, including the *Government Action Regulation*.

4.4 The level of forest retention for the Special Value Areas shown in Attachment A is 100%.

4.5 Upon signing this Land Use Agreement, Provincial representatives will initiate the following actions for the areas identified as having monumental, archaeological and cultural cedar forest resource value to the Haida (shown in Attachment C), and marbled murrelet nesting habitat value (shown in Attachment D):

    a) Continue Part 13 designations for the areas shown in Attachments C and D under the *Forest Act* for a period of two years from the date of signing of the Agreement; and

    b) Complete Detailed Strategic Planning to determine more precise boundaries and establish legal land use objectives for the areas shown in Attachments C and D, to determine the level of forest harvesting consistent with maintenance of monumental, archaeological and cultural cedar forest resource values and marbled murrelet values.

5.0 Ecosystem Based Management (EBM) Objectives

5.1 The EBM Objectives identified in Attachment B through collaborative planning will be used to guide forest planning and related harvesting activities in the Operating Area shown on Attachment A.

5.2 Components of the EBM Objectives in Attachment B will be the subject of further analysis and development by the Parties into land use objectives that will be established by the Province in accordance with the *Land Use Objectives Regulation* made under the *Land Act*.

5.3 The Haida will establish the EBM Objectives in accordance with their laws, policies, customs, traditions and decision making processes.

6.0 Social and Economic Considerations

6.1 In consideration of its potential socio-economic and community implications, the Parties commit to achieving an initial timber harvest opportunity of no less than 800,000 m3/year through the implementation of this Land Use Agreement.

6.2 The Parties agree to assess the Land Use Zones as shown in Attachment A during detailed strategic planning and implementation of this Land Use Agreement, to determine any additional means of achieving the ecological, cultural, social and economic considerations reflected in this Agreement.

6.3 The Parties agree to develop a process that will inform the determination of the long-term timber supply for Haida Gwaii.

7.0 Implementation Structures

7.1 Upon the effective date of this Land Use Agreement, the Parties will establish the structures for implementation and monitoring of this Agreement, including implementation of EBM as outlined in Attachment E.

8.0   Implementation

8.1   This Land Use Agreement will be implemented by the Haida in accordance with their laws, policies, customs, traditions and their decision making processes and authorities.

8.2   This Agreement will be implemented by the Province in accordance with its laws, policies, and decision making processes and authorities.

8.3   The Parties will collaborate in the finalization of New Protected Area boundaries. The boundaries will exclude, where possible, existing mineral tenures, areas with high mineral potential, and ecotourism lodges and provide for their access. Where required, the Parties will consider provision for corridors to access future power development and to prevent isolation or cut-off of adjacent land and resource tenures.

8.4   The Parties will collaborate in the development of management agreements and plans for New Protected Areas.

8.5   The Parties will collaborate in the development of marine foreshore and nearshore planning to address uses and activities compatible with New Protected Areas.

8.6   The Parties will collaborate in the development of Detailed Strategic Plans to determine the most appropriate designations and specific boundaries for the Special Value Areas shown in Attachment A, and to test adapt (where necessary) and apply the EBM objectives identified in Attachment B.

8.7   Upon signing of this Land Use Agreement, the Parties will formulate a joint work plan and collaborate on the achievement of the following tasks:

     a)   Resolution of final, detailed boundaries for New Protected Areas;

     b)   Establishment of an implementation monitoring committee and EBM working group;

     c)   Management planning for New Protected Areas and associated foreshore and nearshore planning);

     d)   Detailed Strategic Planning and adapting (where necessary) of the EBM Objectives in this Land Use Agreement;

     e)   Negotiation of collaborative management agreements for New Protected Areas;

     f)   Legal designation of the New Protected Areas;

     g)   Establishment of land use objectives for forest management under provincial statute and delete Part 13 areas;

     h)   Designation of the Special Value Areas under the appropriate Provincial legislative mechanisms; and

     i)   Completion of New Protected Area management planning and associated marine foreshore and nearshore planning.

8.8   The Parties acknowledge that the successful implementation of this Land Use Agreement depends on the dedication of adequate human and financial resources to cooperatively undertake the activities described in this Agreement.

9.0   Term of Agreement

9.1   This Land Use Agreement takes effect on the date that it is signed by the Parties ("effective date").

9.2   On the effective date, the Parties will each name a contact, to be jointly responsible for overseeing the implementation activities identified in this Land Use Agreement and the preparation of detailed work plans and budget for approval by the Parties.

9.3   The Parties may agree to initiate the review of this Land Use Agreement, including its attachments, upon written request by either Party.

10.0 General Provisions

10.1 This Land Use Agreement is not a treaty or a lands claims agreement within the meaning of section 25 and 35 of the *Constitution Act, 1982* and does not define, amend, recognize, affirm, deny or limit the aboriginal rights, aboriginal title, or treaty rights of the Haida Nation.

10.2 Except as the Parties may otherwise agree in writing, this Land Use Agreement will not limit or prejudice the positions that either Party may take in future negotiations or court actions.

10.3 This Land Use Agreement does not change or affect the positions either Party has, or may have, regarding its jurisdiction, responsibilities and/or decision-making authority, nor is it to be interpreted in a manner that would affect or unlawfully interfere with that decision-making authority.

10.4 Nothing in this Land Use Agreement limits or defines the consultation and accommodation obligations between the Haida and the Province.

This Land Use Agreement signed on the _____ day of _____, 2007 by:

_____

Guujaaw
President,
Council of the Haida Nation

_____

Honourable Gordon Campbell
Premier,
Province of British Columbia

The signing of this Land Use Agreement witnessed by:

_____

Arnie Bellis
Vice President,
Haida Nation

_____

Honourable Pat Bell
Minister of Agriculture and Lands,
Province of British Columbia

ATTACHMENT A

LAND USE ZONES AND ATTRIBUTES

LAND USE ZONE ATTRIBUTES

NEW PROTECTED AREAS

- Areas set aside for ecological and cultural conservation, spiritual and recreational purposes
- Areas maintained for benefit, education and enjoyment of present and future generations
- Provision to be made in the finalization of boundaries for exclusion, where possible, of existing mineral tenures, areas with high mineral potential, and ecotourism lodges and for their access.
- Provision to be made in the finalization of boundaries for corridors, where required, to access future power development and to prevent isolation or cut-off of adjacent land and resource tenures.

OPERATING AREAS

- Areas identified for continued resource development and management activities, including forest harvesting and forest management in accordance with Ecosystem Based Management Objectives.
- Provision for non-forestry resource and land development.
- Provision to be made for continuation of existing industrial access routes, and for establishment of new routes where required to access resource and land tenures.

SPECIAL VALUE AREAS

- Areas identified as having value as areas of critical nesting habitat for goshawk, great blue heron, and saw-whet owl.
- Provision to be made in the finalization of boundaries for corridors, where required, to access future power development and to prevent isolation or cut-off of adjacent land and resource tenures.
- The amount of forest retention in Special Value Areas is 100%.

ATTACHMENT B

ECOSYSTEM BASED MANAGEMENT OBJECTIVES FOR HAIDA GWAII

Part I

1.0 GENERAL

1.1   The Parties acknowledge flexibility may be required in developing or implementing Ecosystem Based Management (EBM) Objectives in situations where:

   a)   The landscapes to which the proposed EBM Objectives apply have already been altered to a significant extent; and

   b)   There is an emerging or previously unforeseen imbalance between environmental, cultural and socio-economic conditions

1.2   Accordingly, these EBM Objectives may incorporate a "default target", a "risk-managed target" or both, as currently set out in this document.

1.3   Either Party or any third party can propose that an operational plan utilize the "risk-managed target" in accordance with the provisions set out in these EBM Objectives (Attachment B).

1.4   Where a third party proposes to utilize a risk managed target, the Parties will review the request based on the following requirements:

   a)   The resource value that is being risk managed must be protected or sustained;

   b)   Adaptive Management principles are applied;

   c)   The purpose for taking the risk managed approach warrants consideration.

2.0 RELATIONSHIP BETWEEN THE PARTIES

2.1   The Parties will implement these EBM Objectives in accordance with any results arising from the shared decision-making discussions being undertaken between the Parties. Decisions will be made on the basis of the Parties obtaining all appropriate and adequate information, in order to make an informed decision.

3.0 RELATIONSHIP WITH FOREST TENURE HOLDERS

3.1   Prior to the implementation of the legal objectives, the Province will work with the Haida to enable forest tenure holders and BC Timber Sales to work towards, on a voluntary basis, implementation of the EBM Management Objectives.

3 2   The Parties will engage in discussions with forest tenure holders to facilitate cooperation and the sharing of appropriate and adequate information.

4.0   AMENDMENT

4.1   These EBM Objectives may be amended by mutual agreement of the Parties. All amendments must be consistent with EBM principles and address the following criteria:

a) Protection of Haida cultural heritage values;

b) Maintenance of ecological integrity and socio-economic balance over the long term;

c) Provision for corrective measures if future monitoring indicates loss of important cultural or ecological values.

Part II

1.0   MANAGEMENT OBJECTIVES

1.1 **Class of Management Objective**: Haida traditional forest resources and
traditional heritage features.

Objective	Measure/Indicator	Targets	Comments/Management Considerations
Identify and maintain Haida traditional forest resources	Preparation and implementation of stewardship strategies for Haida traditional forest resources	Maintain traditional forest resources in sufficient amounts to support Haida Food Social and Ceremonial use of the forest.	Province to work with Haida to prepare Detailed Strategic Plans to identify and maintain adequate traditional forest resources. Harvest strategies within areas shown on Attachment C will be designed to maintain the integrity of traditional cedar forest resources.
Identify and protect Haida traditional heritage features	Number of identified Haida Nation traditional heritage features and sites protected.	Discussions with the Haida in accordance with Section 2 are required before traditional heritage features and sites are altered or removed.	Include a management zone sufficient to maintain the integrity of the feature or site. Province to work with Haida to prepare Detailed Strategic Plans to reserve traditional heritage features.

1.2   Class of Management Objective: Monumental Cedar.

Objective	Measure/Indicator	Targets	Comments/Management Considerations
Identify and maintain Monumental Cedar for Haida cultural use.	Number of identified Monumental Cedar reserved or provided to Haida.	Sufficient volume and quality to support Haida present and future cultural use.	"Monumental Cedar" is defined as a visibly sound red or yellow cedar tree that is greater than 100cm dbh and has a log 7 metres or longer above the flare with at least one face that is suitable for cultural use. This definition may be refined to better reflect the requirements for Monumental Cedar. Identify the location and abundance of Monumental Cedar during timber reconnaisance, cruise and engineering operational planning phases, and seek to identify key areas of potential during Detailed Strategic Planning. Criteria for the consideration of alteration or removal of Monumental Cedar will be developed by the Parties.
	Measure/Indicator	**Targets**	**Comments/Management Considerations**
Sustain stands of Monumental Cedar	Hectares of stands with confirmed presence of Monumental Cedar protected Hectares of stands with a high probability of producing Monumental Cedar protected	Maintain an ongoing supply of Monumental Cedar in sufficient amount to support Haida Social and Ceremonial use	Stands containing Monumental Cedar may be confirmed through Detailed Strategic Plans or operational planning Licensees should map and reserve those stands from harvest, including a management zone and appropriate boundary Reserves may be formally designated in old growth reserves or incorporated in other landscape and watershed reserves Areas outlined in Attachment C will be assessed through Detailed Strategic Planning to determine their suitability as Monumental Cedar reserves. Wherever possible a Monumental Cedar reserve should overlap other landscape level reserves

1.3 Class of Management Objective: Western yew, western red and yellow cedar.

Objective	Measure/Indicator	Targets	Comments/Management Considerations
Retain cedar and yew within harvest units.	Abundance, size and age of cedar and yew retained in harvest units.	Aggregate retention patches: retain cedar in a range of diameters and abundance generally representative of the pre-harvest stand. 100% retention of yew except where alteration or harvesting is required for road access, other infrastructure or to address a safety concern.	Use timber reconnaissance and cruise data to design aggregate retention patches to maintain cedar. In landscapes and watersheds where cedar is significantly reduced below the natural profile, retention should focus on maintaining a higher representation of old and mature cedar.
Maintain a supply of cedar and yew for cultural/social purposes in the bioregion.	Hectares available and managed for Haida cultural / ceremonial use.	Maintain a supply of cedar and yew in sufficient amounts to support Haida Social and Ceremonial use. Discussions with the Haida required to determine target.	Areas outlined on Attachment C will be assessed through Detailed Strategic Planning to determine their suitability as cedar stewardship areas. Specific harvest strategies will be developed within cedar stewardship areas in order to maintain integrity of cedar values. Ensure a natural abundance of cedar and yew is maintained to "free to grow" in harvested areas.

1.4   Class of Management Objective: Culturally modified trees (CMTs).

Objective	Measure/Indicator	Targets	Comments/Management Considerations
Identify and protect culturally modified trees	Number of individual CMTs protected.	Default target: 100% Risk managed target: Discussions with the Haida are required in accordance with Section 2	A culturally modified tree (CMT) is a tree that has been modified by Haida people as part of their cultural use of the forests. CMTs that are reserved will have a management zone sufficient to maintain the integrity of the feature. CMTs and associated windfirm buffer will become a component of stand-level retention. Criteria for alteration or removal of CMTs will be developed by the Parties.
Reserve culturally modified tree areas.	Number of CMT Areas protected and placed in long-term reserves.	Default target: 100% Risk managed target: Discussions with the Haida in accordance with Section 2	A "CMT Area/Archeological forest" is where more than 3 CMTs are all found in close proximity to one another, and includes a management zone of sufficient width to maintain the integrity of the CMT Area. Areas outlined in Attachment C will be assessed through Detailed Strategic Planning to determine suitability as CMT Areas. Specific harvest strategies will be developed to maintain the integrity of CMT values. CMT Areas reserved from harvest will be designated within "Old Growth Management Areas" (OGMAs), in-stand retention or other landscape and watershed reserves. Designation of CMT Areas may require adjustment to accommodate other landscape level reserves.

1.5   Class of Management Objective: Aquatic habitats.

Objective	Measure/Indicator	Targets	Comments/Management Considerations
Maintain and / or restore water quality and quantity within the natural range of variability in identified sensitive watersheds.	"Equivalent Clearcut Area "(ECA) within the forested land base in each watershed	Default: 20% Risk-Managed: Based on CWAP or Watershed Sensitivity Assessment.	Risk managed proposals should be developed cooperatively with the Parties. Initial sensitive watersheds are: Ain, Awun, Bonanza, Copper, Davidson, Deena, Mamin, Mathers, Naden, Riley and some sub-basins of the Yakoun watersheds (Lower Yakoun, Canyon, Upper Yakoun, Phantom, Ghost, King, Gold, Florence). Additional sensitive watersheds to be considered during Detailed Strategic Planning. Further analysis of ECA will be completed prior to development of legal objectives.

Objective	Measure/Indicator	Targets	Comments/Management Considerations
Maintain the natural ecological function of high value fish habitat	Per cent reduction in the natural amount of old riparian forest within 2.0 tree lengths of streams, lakes, wetlands and estuaries classified as high value fish habitat.	Default: 0% Risk-managed: 5%	Buffer widths may vary +/- 0.5 tree heights to address site specific values, including critical habitat for Species at Risk not otherwise reserved. Detailed Strategic Plans should consider the recruitment of second growth riparian forest to restore functional riparian forest in areas previously harvested. High value fish habitat means critical* spawning and rearing areas for anadromous and non anadromous fish including: a) estuaries (including eel grass beds, and salmonid rearing areas); b) wet flood plains (including main channel salmonid spawning habitats, and off channel habitat used for rearing and spawning); and c) marine interface areas (including, shallow intertidal areas, kelp beds, herring spawn areas, and other nearshore habitats used by marine invertebrates for reproduction and rearing). *The Parties agree to further develop, refine and adapt the definition of "critical" as appropriate for Haida Gwaii during Detailed Strategic Planning.
Maintain the natural ecological function of S1-S3 streams, lakes, marsh and fen wetlands not classified as high value fish habitat.	% reduction in the natural amount of mature or old riparian forest within 1.5 tree lengths of feature	Default: 10% Risk-managed: 20 %	Buffer widths may vary +/- 0.5 tree heights to address site specific values, including critical habitat for Species at Risk not otherwise reserved. Recruit functional riparian forest in areas previously harvested. Minimum size of lakes marshes and fen wetland (0.25 – 1.0 ha) to be developed through further analysis.
Retain Active Fluvial Units.	% reduction in the natural amount of mature plus old riparian forest within 1.5 tree lengths from the outer edge of Active Fluvial Units.	Default: 10% Risk-managed: 20%	Buffer widths may vary +/- 0.5 tree heights to address site specific values, including critical habitat for Species at Risk not otherwise reserved. "Active Fluvial Units" are defined as all active floodplains where water flows overland in a normal flood event, and includes low and medium bench and the hydro-geomorphic riparian zone of all active fans. Recruit functional riparian forest in areas previously harvested.

Objective	Measure/Indicator	Targets	Comments/Management Considerations
Maintain the natural ecological function of upland streams.	% reduction in the natural amount of Functional Riparian Forest	Default: 30% Risk-Managed Based on CWAP or Watershed Sensitivity Assessment	"Functional Riparian Forest" is defined as forest that has reached "Hydrologically Effective Greenup" (HEG), and also contains some large trees adjacent to streams for recruitment of "Large Organic Debris" (LOD). Upland streams are defined as Class 4 to 6 streams that have a slope greater than 5%. Retention should be designed to encompass: a) streams with unique microclimate; b) streams with other rare ecological or geomorphological characteristics, including high-density; and c) first-order streams.
Retain forested swamps	% reduction in the natural amount of mature plus old riparian forest within 1.5 tree lengths of forested swamps	Watershed Target Default: 30% Risk-managed: 40%	Buffer widths may vary +/- 0.5 tree heights to address site specific values, including critical habitat for Species at Risk not otherwise reserved. "Forested Swamps" means a forested mineral wetland or forested peatland with standing or gently flowing nutrient rich water in pools or channels and the water table is usually at or near the surface of the wetland or peatland. It does not include poorly drained areas transitional to uplands where: a) folisolic growing substrate (i.e. folic material derived from the litter of trees and lesser vegetation of upland sites) occupies 50% or more of the site area; or b) hydromorphic organic matter (organic material accumulated under saturated conditions) and wetland species hydrophytes occupy less than 50% of the site area. Recruit functional riparian forest in areas previously harvested. Minimum size of forested swamps (0.25 – 1.0 ha) to be developed through further analysis.

1.6 Class of Management Objective: Biodiversity.

Objective	Measure/Indicator	Targets	Management Considerations
Maintain representation of common and very common old forest ecosystems in the bioregion.	Proportion (%) of each very common and common site series by BEC variant that exists in natural old growth condition.	Bioregion target. Maintain greater than 30% of the natural proportion of old forest within each site series/BEC variant.	Allocation of higher management targets to specific landscapes and watersheds may be done during development of Detailed Strategic Plans. Site series (or their surrogates) and site series groupings, the natural proportion of old forest in each site series, and the ages that each site series are considered old, will be defined by the Parties.
Maintain representation of modal, rare and very rare old forest ecosystems in the bioregion.	Proportion (%) of each modal, uncommon and rare site series by BEC variant that exists in natural old growth condition.	Bioregion target. Maintain greater than 70% of the natural proportion within each site series/BEC variant.	The standard for assessing site series is the best available of "Predictive Ecosystem Mapping" (PEM), "Terrestrial Ecosystem Mapping" (TEM) or forest cover/"Biogeoclimatic Ecosystem Classification"(BEC) surrogate, whichever is available for the area of interest (i.e. the landscape unit or watershed). Targets for old forest retention or recruitment outside of protection areas may be met through: old growth stands outside the "Timber Harvesting Land Base" (THLB); retention within harvested stands; spatial/temporal scheduling of forestry activities; and zoning of "Old Growth Management Areas" (OGMAs). Further analysis of old forest representation targets will be completed prior to development of legal objectives. Where there is less than the bioregion area target for a site series, design recruitment strategies to meet the target within 250 years. Design OGMAs to address old seral objectives, whether on or off the THLB, to protect critical habitat for "Species At Risk" (SAR) and regionally important wildlife including: a) Northern Goshawks (nesting areas and post fledgling habitat); b) Black bear den sites; c) Marbled Murrelets, Great Blue herons, Saw Whet owls (nesting habitat).

Objective	Measure/Indicator	Targets	Management Considerations
Identify and protect red-listed plant communities	% reduction of individual red listed plant communities identified by the Parties.	Default: 0% Risk managed 5%	Default target should only be exceeded if required for access or safety. The standard for assessing/measuring site series is the best of PEM, TEM or BEC/forest cover, whichever is available. Existence of red listed plant communities on the ground should be confirmed prior to operations commencing. List of red-listed plant communities to be developed through Detailed Strategic Planning.
Identify and protect selected blue-listed plant communities	% reduction of the blue-listed plant communities identified by the Parties.	Default: 0% Risk Managed 30%	The standard for assessing / measuring site series is the best of PEM, TEM or BEC / forest cover, whichever is available. Existence of blue listed plant communities on the ground should be confirmed prior to operations commencing. List of blue-listed plant communities to be developed through Detailed Strategic Planning.

1.7   Management Objective: Wildlife habitat.

Objective	Measure/Indicator	Targets	Management Considerations
Identify and protect black bear den sites.	Number of den sites protected.	Default 100%	Include a windfirm management area of 1ha. Bear dens are sites which show evidence of current or past use by bears. Criteria for alteration or removal of den sites include: a) where alteration or removal is required for access, or b) where retention of all den sites would make harvesting the cutblock economically unviable. Retain suitable structure in cutblocks for retention and recruitment of denning habitat through time. Manage for old growth recruitment in second growth forests and identify potential Western Red cedar and Cypress trees as future dens.
Maintain Marbled Murrelet nesting habitat.	Alteration of Class 1 and 2 habitat by landscape unit	Default: Maximum 10 % alteration of class 1 Default: Maximum 30% alteration of class 2	Retain habitat through protected areas, landscape level reserves, and the use of alternative silviculture systems. Areas outlined in Attachment D will be assessed through Detailed Strategic Planning to determine suitability as Marbled Murrelet nesting habitat. Specific harvest strategies will be developed to maintain the integrity of Marbled Murrelet nesting values. Spatial location of nesting habitat to be retained within the Operating Area shown in Attachment A will be defined through Detailed Strategic Planning and analysis.
Identify and protect goshawk nesting sites.	Number of nest sites protected	Default 100%	Protect known northern goshawk nest sites within a reserve of approximately 200 hectares.

ATTACHMENT C

MAP OF MONUMENTAL, ARCHAEOLOGICAL AND CULTURAL CEDAR
FOREST RESOURCE VALUE AREAS

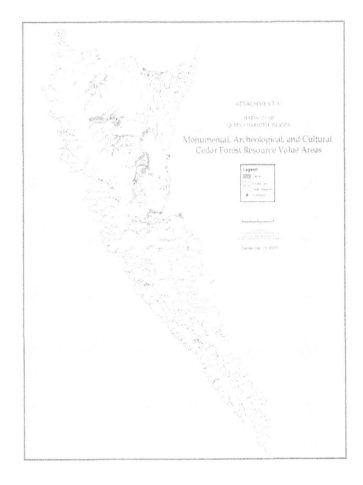

ATTACHMENT D

MAP OF MARBLED MURRELET NESTING HABITAT

ATTACHMENT E

STRUCTURES FOR IMPLEMENTING THE FINAL LAND USE AGREEMENT

1.0 Government to Government Relationship:

1.1 The Parties will implement EBM and this Land Use Agreement, monitor progress on implementation, and consider further agreements related to land use planning.

1.2 Where the Parties agree, aspects of this Agreement may be implemented by working through the Coastal First Nations Land and Resource Forum on specific matters including:

   a) Development and implementation of cooperative economic initiatives and policies that will enable the Haida and the communities of Haida Gwaii to achieve their social and economic objectives;

   b) Other relevant activities outlined in the Coastal First Nations' *Land and Resource Protocol* established as part of the Coast Land Use Announcement of February 2006. For greater clarity, the Parties will determine the relevancy and consistency of the *Land and Resource Protocol* with this Land Use Agreement.

2.0 Plan Implementation Monitoring Committee:

2.1 The Parties will develop a Terms of Reference and establish an advisory committee with representation from the Island Community to monitor the implementation of this Land Use Agreement.

3.0 Ecosystem Based Management Working Group:

3.1 The Parties will develop a Terms of Reference and establish an advisory committee to make recommendations on the further development, monitoring and implementation of EBM on Haida Gwaii.

3.2 The Haida may participate on the Coast-wide EBM Working Group established as part of the Coast Land Use Announcement of February 2006.

APPENDIX 3:

Haida Land Use Vision

HAIDA LAND USE VISION

HAIDA GWAII YAH'GUUDANG
[respecting Haida Gwaii]

Council of the Haida Nation
April 2005

Council of the Haida Nation — Haida Land Use Vision

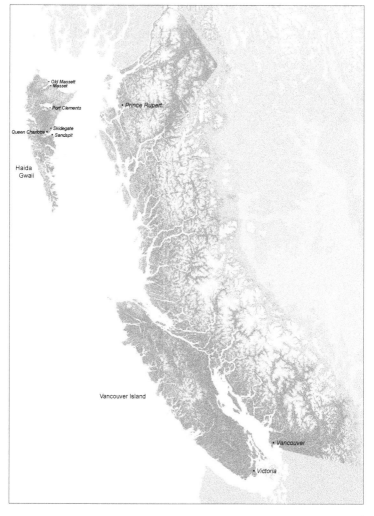

Haida Gwaii Yah'guudang — respecting Haida Gwaii

he Haida Nation is the rightful heir to Haida Gwaii.

Our culture, our heritage, is the child of respect and intimacy with the land and sea.

Like the forests, the roots of our people are intertwined such that the greatest troubles cannot overcome us.

We owe our existence to Haida Gwaii.

The living generation accepts the responsibility to ensure that our heritage is passed on to following generations.

On these islands our ancestors lived and died, and here too   we will make our homes until called away to join them in the great beyond.

from the Constitution of the Haida Nation

3

The Haida Land Use Vision

This vision represents an attempt to balance the ecological, cultural and economic interests on Haida Gwaii. While a comprehensive plan would have been better enacted 40 or 100 years ago when there was more to work with industrial development met with little resistance. Without this plan, this generation will have witnessed the last of the ancient forests and for that matter we will have seen the end of our culture.

We know that up to this year, logging companies have been cutting the nesting areas of the night birds. We know that they have been logging cedar on double shifts and the only planning has been to turn the trees into logs and divide up the loot. Their intention was to start with the best timber and log it and to keep logging until it was all gone, then start again and log the next crop until that was gone.

Over time it has become apparent that by stripping the watersheds, the salmon spawning habitat of the salmon and seabirds were being wiped out. It was also clear that cedar, the very foundation of our culture, would be wiped out.

We have brought together the efforts of the past 30 years where the Haida Nation has identified areas that must be protected, in addition we have set aside a sizeable amount of the remaining cedar and the sacred workplaces of our ancestors, identified through the work of the Forest Guardians.

Essentially, more than half of the islands will remain in the state that our ancestors knew and with planning and care, we can exercise another 1000 years and more of culture. The Haida Land Use Vision has been adopted by all representatives of the Planning Table except the forest industry, while the Province remained nuetral. The values and principles brought forward in this document are sound and defendable at every level, and will provide a level of comfort we have not enjoyed for the past 100 years. It will also provide the follwoing generations options they would not otherwise realize. For this generation, we can hold our heads up and know that we have taken the right steps in our day. •

Foreword to the VISION

The common name for these islands is *Haida Gwaii* meaning *people island* or *island of the people*. In earlier times this place was more commonly known as *Haadala Gwaii-ai,* meaning *taken out of concealment.* At the time of *Nangkilslas* it was *Didakwaa Gwaii,* meaning *shoreward country.*

Our oral history traces the lineage of our families back to our ocean origins. We've witnessed the ice age, two great floods, changes in the sea level, the arrival of the first tree and many other earth-changing events. Together with all living things we've grown and prospered through the ages, nourished by the wealth and generosity of the ocean around us.

Our physical and spiritual relationship with the lands and waters of Haida Gwaii, our history of co-existence with all living things over many thousands of years is what makes up Haida culture. *Yah'guudang* — our respect for all living things — celebrates the ways our lives and spirits are intertwined and honors the responsibility we hold to future generations.

Yah'guudang is about respect and responsibility, about knowing our place in the web of life, and how the fate of our culture runs parallel with the fate of the ocean, sky and forest people.

Our people are thankful of our place in this world. Our stories, songs, dances and crests are displayed through the ancient traditions of feasting and potlatching, where prestige is gained through the distribution of property. Handed down in private or displayed in the formal array of our traditions, they weave together through time the historic fabric of Haida Gwaii. •

4

Haida Gwaii Yah'guudang — respecting Haida Gwaii

THE HAIDA LAND USE VISION

From the beginning of time and counted in many generations, the Haida Nation has adapted to the changing earth. The art forms associated with Haida culture and celebrated for being among the world's great intellectual accomplishments, is an expression of our relationship to Haida Gwaii.

the well-being of the land. We need to clearly understand the changes that have occurred in ecological conditions and our culture, and then provide directions for restoring and maintaining balance. The HLUV considers the land and forests, rivers and lakes, and the life that inhabits them, in

Over the past fifty years, the lands and waters have been impoverished by over-exploitation. The corporate bonanza has come at the cost of the culture and communities. There has been no comprehensive planning or regulation other than the extraction of resources and revenues to feed the insatiable appetites of an economy and people who don't live here and are not concerned with the consequences of their actions.

Today we recognize that the resource industries have gone too far too fast, and that important cultural, economic and environmental issues need to be addressed. For this reason, the Council of the Haida Nation and province of British Columbia convened a strategic land use planning process, now underway. The Haida Land Use Vision is a foundation of the process, produced by the Council of the Haida Nation to guide the Community Planning Forum and other deliberations towards a sustainable Land Use Plan for Haida Gwaii.

The Haida Land Use Vision (HLUV) reflects our understanding of how things function together and how they have changed through time. It conveys our concern about the damage that has occurred in recent times, and addresses the need to ensure continuity and sustainability for the generations to come.

To sustain Haida culture, a land use plan must adequately address certain priorities, beginning with

particular the cedar, salmon, bear, birds and plants that matter to Haida culture. We describe some of what we know about them, why they are important and how we are connected.

The Haida Land Use Vision is a living document. This draft has been developed by the Council and people of the Haida Nation for presentation to the Community Planning Forum in May of 2004. It has gone through many changes in preparation, and we expect that over the next several months, the text and maps will be revised to include new information from the communities and Land Use Plan process.

It should be noted that the planning process is limited to the land, even though the land and ocean are linked together in many ways. This document addresses all the places where people go on land,

5

from hilltops to the low tide beaches. In time, when a marine planning process occurs, the ocean and all that it entails will be given full consideration.

Finally, this document is based on Haida culture — the land use vision it describes is based on Yah'guudang. We appreciate that people from other cultures also have attachments to this sacred place, and seek to work together in harmony and accord.

our place

Haida Gwaii is an island, lodged in the northeast corner of the Pacific Ocean. It's an isolated archipelago of forest, muskeg and ocean, shaped like a bear's canine tooth shrouded in swirling clouds. The closest landfalls are about eighty kilometers away on the mainland west coast of Canada, and the bottom of the Alaska panhandle where the *Kiis Haada* live.

The land was formed by ancient upheavals, volcanoes, sediments, ice flows and runoff. The surrounding ocean climate is warmer than the neighboring mainland, so during the ice ages some parts of the islands remained free of glaciers.

Most of the modern Hecate Strait and parts of our outer coastal regions were once above sea level, covered by tundra, streams and lakes, and inhabited by our ancestors. Over just the past few thousand years, the sea level has fluctuated by almost two hundred metres, while the fish, forest life and our people adapted to the changing times.

The weather is shaped by the dynamics of the largest ocean on earth: there are high winds and rain, large

tides, mild winter temperatures and cool, cloudy summers. Warm ocean currents mix with cold water upwellings rich in nutrients. The sea is abundant in plankton, sea-weeds, fish, shellfish and mammals. Through the lives of everyone — people, seabirds and salmon, bear, and many others — the food webs of the ocean and land are woven tightly together.

Because of our isolation, unique forms of life have evolved — birds, mammals, fish, plants and insects — in plenty. The forests are renowned for growing trees of high quality, for large seabird nesting colonies, unique salmon populations, raptors, the world's largest black bears, and an abundance of diverse ocean life. This is the physical and biological world in which Haida culture has grown for thousands of years, ever since Raven coaxed the first people from a cockle shell. •

Part One

Council of the Haida Nation — Haida Land Use Vision

Part One
This part of the HLUV describes some of the key things about the land
and waters that have a special place in Haida culture. The list is not
meant to be complete, but it does address many aspects of our relations
with Haida Gwaii. It includes:

Tsuuaay, *cedar*

Tsiin, *salmon*

Taan, *black bear*

Xiit'lit, *birds*

Kil, *plants*

Sk'waii, *beach*

Considering each in turn,
we present some details of
our collective understanding
of how things are inter-
connected and why they're
important.

Tsuuaay—Cedar
Our stories begin in the time
before cedar, when living
conditions were more basic.
They tell of the intervention
of supernaturals in the birth
of canoe technology, and of the first totem poles being seen in an
underwater village.

Tsuuaay arrived on Haida Gwaii about six thousand years ago. In
time it became an essential part of Haida culture, and the products
of our cedar technology fill many volumes of books, display cases
and collections around the world. Today as ever, the cedar tree is
essential to Haida well-being — which includes material things and
cultural affairs as well as growing economic opportunities in forest
manage-ment, logging, carving and construction. The renewal and
strength of Haida culture is intimately linked to the well-being of
tsuuaay.

Cedar trees are important to many other living things great and
small. They provide habitat for forest creatures, some of which are
an important feature of Haida crests and histories. The biggest one
is *taan*, the black bear, taking shelter and giving birth in hollow, dry
cedar trees. Smaller, but as important to the forest, are the birds, bats
and others that nest and perch in cedar trees. As insect-eaters and

A cedar forest near Juskatla Inlet.

seed spreaders, they help to maintain healthy forest conditions, which includes hunting opportunities for predatory birds and mammals.

When a Haida person goes for bark, a pole or a canoe, trees are approached with respect. Their spirits are hailed in a song and thanked with prayer. A bark gatherer takes care that the tree will go on living. A canoe builder *looks into the heart* of a cedar (test holes) so that trees with unsuitable qualities will be left standing alive much as before. The Culturally Modified Trees (CMTs) and canoe blanks that you find in the forest are the sacred workplaces of our ancestors.

the condition of tsuuaay

For several decades the Haida have voiced growing concerns that the high rate of cedar logging is threatening the continuity of Haida culture, both today and especially for the coming generations. Cedar of high quality for canoes, poles and longhouses are disappearing from Haida Gwaii within *our* lifetime, cut down and floated away on log barges at a rate out of all proportion to their number. The needs of future artists, communities, bears and other forest dwellers are not respected by government planners and professional foresters.

The problem is compounded by the large population of introduced deer, which has reduced the ability of cedar to grow back after logging, and even in the old growth forest that remains.

The young cedar stands in the 19th century burn area between the lower Yakoun and Tlell rivers need special consideration. Some of them grow in very rich soil, and three hundred years from now they'll be one of the few remaining sources of accessible monumental cedars — if they aren't logged out in the next decade.

"Cedar of high quality for canoes, poles and longhouses are disappearing from Haida Gwaii within our lifetime, cut down and floated away on log barges at a rate out of all proportion to their number. The needs of future artists, communities, bears and other forest dwellers are not respected by government planners and professional foresters."

Tsiin—Salmon

Salmon are integral to all life on Haida Gwaii and to Haida culture. We express this understanding in our art forms when the salmon-trout-head design is placed in the ovoid joints of other creatures.

There are races of salmon and other fish on Haida Gwaii that are ancient and unique in the world. The sockeye return much earlier than other parts of the mainland coast. There are land-locked salmon in various lakes, the outcome of changing sea levels.

Every year the salmon swim into the forest to spawn, carrying in their bodies thousands of tonnes of nutrients gathered in ocean food

"Salmon are creatures of the forest, they're born there and they die there."

Charles F. Bellis

Detail for argillite platter, about 1885.

Council of the Haida Nation — Haida Land Use Vision

webs, back to the land. They feed everything on the way upstream and down. They are the single most important source of nourishment in our diet, and over the years we have developed many ways to prepare, store and serve them in family meals and ceremonial feasts.

Many others also rely on *tsiin* for food. Over time, Black bear snatch tens of thousands of salmon out of the streams and bring nutrients to the forest floor. Many times they eat choice parts and leave the rest to be eaten by birds, small mammals and insects.

Eventually the nutrients within the salmon pass into the soil and from there to the roots of trees and plants. The salmon feed the forest and in return receive clean water and gravel in which to hatch and grow, sheltered from extremes of temperature and water flow in times of high and low rainfall.

"It is clear that the provincial Forest Practices Code is a case of too little, too late. It provides no protection for the thousands of small stream habitats, or the vital headwaters of streams where much logging is happening today."

the condition of tsiin
Years of habitat disruption and overfishing is evident in all our streams. Sockeye in particular are in dire straits compared to their historical abundance. Every year we have to carefully limit our catches in different rivers so as not to endanger them. At times we find there's not enough to go around to provide for the needs of single families, let alone large public feasting.

As a watershed becomes progressively logged, the qualities that make for a healthy salmon stream become degraded. In many places the riparian forest that surrounds the streams and lakes has been laid bare. Because the hillside forests have been taken as well, seasonal floods run faster and higher, ripping away the structure of logs and spawning pools and the shelter of small side channels. Roads and bridge crossings funnel sediments into the streams. Landslides and debris torrents are catastrophic events that effectively erase a stream's capacity to provide habitat.

One of the worst examples is the Ain River, once a major system and important food source; today barren of sockeye. The Copper River is not much better — almost 90 percent of the watershed has been logged. Where the sockeye are a shadow of their former abundance, Creek Woman's wealth has been diminished.

Other major salmon systems in trouble include the Davidson, Naden, Awun, Mamin, Yakoun, Deena and Mathers, with many smaller streams becoming increasingly degraded.

It is clear that the provincial Forest Practices Code is a case of too little, too late. It provides no protection for the thousands of small stream habitats, or the vital headwaters of streams where much logging is happening today.

10

Haida Gwaii Yah'guudang — respecting Haida Gwaii

Taan—Bear

Our Bear Mother Story, which is often depicted as a crest figure on
family poles, explains our long and close relationship with bears.
We are also similar to them in material ways, such as our reliance
on salmon and cedar, and we learned a great deal from them about
plants and their various uses.

Bears play a key role in the well-being
of the land. When they lift salmon out
of the streams each year, they transfer
a great load of nutrients from the ocean
to the forest floor, much to the benefit
of many other kinds of life.

The best kind of forest for a bear
contains lots of cedar trees of the right size with cavities for dens
and daybeds, succulent plants for spring feeding, berries and salmon
streams. This kind of forest grows at lower elevations in valley
bottoms and neighboring slopes.

Top of a staff. Bear head with a land otter
on its back. Made of antler and abalone
- from Kung.

The best bear mother dens are in larger cedars with a cozy chamber
inside sheltered from wind and rain, and a small well-hidden
opening, easy to defend against intruders. Day beds used in warmer
times by male, female and young can be found near streams and
other places where different foods are in season.

A bear mother has five or six trees in her territory, and moves
between them from winter to winter, birth to birth. If she feels
threatened in her den by a roaming male or disturbed by human
industry, she will pick up and move her cubs to another den tree.

the condition of taan

A great many bear den trees and the forest places around them have
been cut down. Experienced local loggers say that for most of the
past 50 years the common practice has been to cut them. Sometimes
loggers are allowed to leave occupied dens until the bears depart.
When a mother with cubs feels threatened by a disturbance, she
packs up and looks for another den.

When bears are stressed this way, or by
developments such as fishing lodges located in
the best places for their foraging, they come out
of the forest — thrashing around and trashing
things in anger.
The pattern of change can be seen by looking
at the age of second growth forests. The places
where the old forest has been logged have lost
whatever big standing cedar trees for bear dens

Bear Mother story in argillite.

11

and daybeds they once contained, and their disappearance from the land has been extensive. This forces the bears to concentrate in old growth remnants, bringing them stress from crowding and depriving the land of the role they play in the salmon nutrient cycle.

In the recent past, the troubles facing bears were compounded by the Department of Fisheries' misguided and now discontinued policy of killing bears because they eat fish. Most recently, their lives are further threatened by a rapid increase in commercial sport hunting, which like catch-and-release sport fisheries are unforgivable exercises in disrespect and disregard for the lives and spirits of creatures we hold to be our relations.

Wild strawberry,

Kil—Plants

Haida plant use is ancient and complex. Many medicines were shown to us by a supernatural woman and others by the birds and other animals such as–*Taan*. The first tree to arrive in Haida Gwaii was the pine tree, which was taken as a crest by the *Xagi Kiigawaii* who wore a pine branch in their hair. Science has recently confirmed that the pine tree was the first to arrive, about 14,000 years ago.

Everyone depends on plants — people, fish, birds, animals and insects — for the same sorts of things, for nourishment and shelter, and everyone has a role to play in their well-being.

Our uses include a wide variety of things made from different parts of trees and plants — root, bark, stem, flower, berry, leaf and branch. They provide us with medicines, food and teas. Pigments and dyes. Materials for the smokehouse, cooking and weaving of clothing, hats, mats and baskets. From them we can make spears, arrows and bows; string and rope; fish hooks, nets and weirs; tool handles and clubs; whistles, rattles and ceremonial adornments.

The wide range of plants we use grow everywhere from deep forest to open muskeg, meadows and shorelines, but the old growth forest contains many important things, including some of the most powerful medicines with proven effects.

Plants and trees are nourished and affected by the ocean. Depending on its proximity to the ocean and exposure to its influence, the   same kind of plant has different qualities for food value and medicinal effect.
Alder plays an important ecological role in the forest. It's one of the first things that grows on the most disturbed sites, and brings nitrogen out of the air and into the nutrient cycle that makes new soil. When alder sees a landslide she exclaims: "I'm going to have that place!"

Haida Gwaii Yah'guudang — respecting Haida Gwaii

Modern drug companies are always searching for natural medicines
to create new commercial opportunities. This commercial
enterprise has caused many problems for traditional
medicine practitioners in many parts of the world, for
which reason we hold our knowledge of these things in
secrecy. They cannot be explained here or shown in any
detail on maps.

the condition of kil
The single-minded focus of the logging industry pays
little regard to the many kinds of plants it calls "non-
timber forest products." No respect is shown for plants
which are sacred to us for their proven medicinal powers
and food values.

Where we might approach a Yew tree in a ceremonial manner,
the industry takes them for building temporary roads, bucked into
pieces for the heavy steel-tracked machines to travel on, then left
behind on the ground.

Drawing of an argillite plate by Charles
Edenshaw. The plate shows the origin of
women with Tree Fungus Man on the left.

Many of the most powerful medicine plants grow in the old growth
forest, especially under the canopy in riparian areas within one
hundred metres of the streams. So much of this kind of forest has
been clearcut that plants like devil's club — also an important
medicine for the bears who taught us to use it — have become very
difficult to find.

Other kinds of plants for food and medicine have become scarce, and
we have to travel further and further to find them. Recently, more
people have become interested in harvesting plants for personal and
commercial use in off-island markets, and this is a growing problem
that needs to be addressed.

Plants and trees are nourished and affected by the ocean. Depending
on their exposure to the ocean's influence, the same kinds of plants
have different nutrient and medicinal properties. Because of this they
need to be protected in various places from the shoreline to more
sheltered inland places.

Xiit'lit—Birds
Many different kinds of birds fly the airways of Haida Gwaii, coming
to ground to swim, bath, perch, eat, rest, sing and nest. Their families
include seabird, songbird, shorebird, falcon, hawk, owl, crow, duck
and goose, sapsucker, woodpecker, kingfisher, heron, swallow, crane,
hummingbird, grouse, loon, gull and cormorant.

13

Through the ages, birds have played an integral role in building and maintaining the well-being of the land and Haida culture. As seed-spreaders, insect-eaters, predators, scavengers and fertilizer carriers, they play a key role in tending the plants in the forest, muskeg, estuary and shoreline what they are.

Seabirds, like salmon, come in from the ocean in great numbers every year to birth their young. They nest in burrows in the ground or mossy platforms in the treetops. Their–*umma* is rich in nitrogen, and over the ages the forests where they nest have grown wealthy with large trees. They are also a part of our traditional diet, an important source of nourishment in the time before the salmon return when stored supplies are running low.

From watching the birds we learned the properties of plants, what is good for nourishment and medicine. Their songs and doings are expressed many different ways, many of which are family crests.

Two of the most prominent birds in Haida culture are the eagle and the raven — which are the crest figures for the two main branches of Haida lineage and social structure. Eagle down is held sacred and is used in ceremony to signify peace and good intentions.

the condition of xiit'lit
Many kinds of birds depend on old growth forests with their high canopies and understories of fern and shrubs such as salal and huckleberry, and plenty of insects to eat. Those who live inside the forest are very vulnerable to disturbance by logging. Clearcuts and the "variable retention" openings are barren of the conditions that birds need to live there, and so their numbers decline.

Rattle - hawk with a frog in its mouth.

The problem is compounded by introduced species. Rats, raccoons and squirrels are alien predators of adult birds, eggs and hatchlings. The growing flocks of starlings are vigorous competitors for the foods that remain. The deer have had the greatest affect, and while we respect that they have become an important part of many people's diet, we need to realize how their heavy browsing of bird and insect habitat has impoverished the plant communities.

Some birds adapt to the new openings and edges that logging creates, but after several years the young conifer forest draws together into a tight canopy that blocks most of the light out from the understory. When this happens, the forests are unsuitable habitat for many birds for up to 60 years, a condition that exists over an ever-increasing portion of the land.

14

Goshawks have declined in number such that they are listed by
the government of British Columbia as a threatened species — the
reason given is the logging of the forests where they nest and
forage. *Ts'alangaa* (Marbled Murrelet) is listed by the province
as a threatened species. Heron and saw whet owls have become
increasingly rare, dependant as they are on old forest conditions for
nesting and foraging.

In effect, the loss of birds is depriving the land of their essential role in
insect control, seed dispersal and nutrient loading, a condition that
will surely become worse if logging continues in the pattern of recent
years.

Shoreline birds are easier to observe, and those who count them say
that the falcons and eagles are still high in number here, in comparison
to the other parts of the mainland.

Argillite pipe, about 1895.

Sk'waii'—Beach

Island dwellers are ocean-going people. In the beginning we came out of
the ocean, and like everything else that inhabits the land we are nourished
and shaped by it — in terms of food, the supernaturals, many stories, the
cycle of the tides, currents and weather, and our use of cedar canoes for
travel, trade and adventure.

In river estuaries large and small, Creek Woman meets the ocean, releasing
the young ones into the beds of eelgrass and kelp forests where they begin
the saltwater stage of their lives, then welcoming them on their return.

The sand and gravel beaches are inhabited by razor clams, butter clams,
horse clams, cockles, geoducks and crabs. On rocky shores are barnacles,
mussels and a multitude of periwinkles, and nourishing seaweeds rich in
minerals and trace elements. Hiding in the seaweed are the abalone, urchin,
scallop and octopus.

The places washed by the ocean's tides are where we go to gather sea foods
of all kinds'— animal, vegetable and mineral. With every tide comes the
nourishment of all living communities.

the condition of sk'waii'

The beaches are vulnerable to disturbance by pollution from human sewage,
oil and the many products made from it, by seepage from mining sites, and
by timber industry activities at log sorting and dumping sites.

Log dumps are usually located in sheltered bays, where bark and debris
sinks to the bottom and decomposes, starving the water of oxygen and
smothering clams and other life forms.

Council of the Haida Nation — Haida Land Use Vision

Wherever streams have been heavily logged and damaged by landslides and erosion, in periods of heavy rainfall the estuaries are loaded with silt and huge quantities of gravel are washed out of the stream channels and into the sea. •

Guulaangw gyaat'aad button robe - orca design. Design by John Yeltatzie, about 1890.

Part Two

Part Two

This part of the HLUV addresses what must be done in accordance with Yah'guudang to bring land and resource use into balance — to ensure the continuity of Haida culture and the economic well-being of the entire Island Community. This part of the document is being worked on as explained below.

On the set of maps, inserted in the centre, we identify places where the land use plan should provide protection against further degradation and address the need to restore things that are damaged.

The map of Haida Protected Areas shows important landscapes that have been brought forward by the Haida Nation in negotiations with the government of British Columbia on interim measures related to the treaty process. There has been little or no logging in these areas over the past ten years, and the province has suspended forestry planning in these places while the process is under way.

Bear Mother - Walker Brown, Skidegate.

Six other maps have been prepared to indicate the scope and intent of measures that need to be taken in order to protect important things that are threatened by continued resource extraction, and to ensure an opportunity for the land to restore and replenish itself. These are:

Tsuuaay, cedar - forests set aside to protect the workplaces of our ancestors and monumental cedars for haida culture.

Tsiin, salmon - riparian forest areas set aside to protect salmon stream conditions and restore degraded watersheds.

Taan, bear - habitat for denning and foraging within their territories where future logging may occur.

Kil, plants - places set aside to protect food and medicine plants.

Xiit'lit, birds - places set aside to protect nesting and foraging habitat.

Sk'waii, beach - places set aside to protect life along the shore and the intertidal zone.

With the exception of the Haida Protected Areas, most of these maps are preliminary in nature. They indicate the scope and intent of the HLUV in restoring balance, but they are not a final determination for use in the Land Use Plan. Good decisions are based on good information, so the completion of these maps will await our review of the report on environmental conditions (still in preparation), and

18

will require further dialogue in the communities and the Planning Forum.

The Haida Land Use Vision is not just about the protection of natural areas. It is also about understanding economic conditions, and providing a vision of a sustainable economy in which the forest continues to play an important role in the well-being of the Island Community.

The forests have fueled an industry that has provided jobs to Haida and other island communities for a few short decades. Families have been fed and sheltered, and relationships among our communities have grown. But the forest was logged too fast, and without provision for the stability and sustainability of the Island Community as a whole.

There is room enough for forestry and other commercial activities on Haida Gwaii, but in order to be sustainable they must be managed with more respect and greater responsibility — in other words, in accordance with yah'guudang.

In Haida culture, wealth is a different thing than money, which is a currency for doing business in the modern economy. Wealth flows from the well-being of the land, and from having the opportunity, knowledge and capacity to support our families, raise healthy children, and organize the individual collective efforts of our clans and society. Wealth is to be shared and distributed — prestige is gained through the ability to do so.

This economic component of the Haida Land Use Vision is also in the works. It will take careful consideration and extensive consultation, and the work towards its completion will proceed in the months ahead.

The land and waters of Haida Gwaii can and must be made well again. Our economic needs can and must be brought into balance with the capacity of the land to function and provide. We have the political will and we accept the responsibility to see that this is done. •

Please note: Colour HLUV maps are available at Band Council offices and the Council of the Haida Nation.

"And know that Haida culture is not simply song and dance,
graven images, stories, language, or even blood. It is all of those things and then…
waking up on Haida Gwaii anticipating the season when the herring spawns.
It is a feeling you get when you bring a feed of cockles to the old people,
and when you are fixing up fish for the smokehouse,
or when walking on barnacles or moss."

HAIDA LAND USE VISION
Council of the Haida Nation
April 2005

APPENDIX 4:

Haida Nation Constitution

Constitution of the Haida Nation

HAIDA PROCLAMATION

"The Haida Nation is the rightful heir to Haida Gwaii. Our culture is born of respect; and intimacy with the land and sea and the air around us. Like the forests, the roots of our people are intertwined such that the greatest troubles cannot overcome us. We owe our existence to Haida Gwaii. The living generation accepts the responsibility to insure that our heritage is passed on to following generations. On these islands our ancestors lived and died and here too, we will make our homes until called away to join them in the great beyond."

SHIP Translation of the Haida Proclamation:
"Iid kuuniisii asii id gii isda gan. Tllgaay ad siigaay G̲an t'alang aax̲ana ad yahguudang. Huu tllguu G̲iidan hlk'inx̲a gaa.ngang x̲aayda hllng.aay gud giijaagids, gaay G̲aaganuu gam gina daaG̲ang.nga id gwii is hllnga G̲ang ga. X̲aaydaG̲a Gwaay.yaay G̲aagamuu iid x̲aynanga ga. Asii gwaay.yaay guu, iid kuuniisii x̲aynang.nga, ad siing.gwaa'ad gan. Sah 'Laana Tllgaay G̲aa id gii k̲yaagang.ngaay G̲aaw aan t'ang naax̲ang sG̲waan.nang G̲as ga. Iid sihlG̲a ga x̲aynangas gii t'alang t'aas.slas, asii k̲yang.gaay llgaay 'waagii kilxii gang ga."

ARTICLE 1   HAIDA TERRITORIES

A1.S1   The Territories of the Haida Nation include the entire lands of Haida Gwaii, the surrounding waters, sub-surface and the air space. The waters include the entire Dixon Entrance, half of the Hecate Straits, halfway to Vancouver Island and Westward into the abyssal ocean depths.

       (a)   The Haida recognizes the independent and separate jurisdiction of the Kaigani Haida.

ARTICLE 2   THE PEOPLE

A2.S1   All people of Haida Ancestry are citizens of the Haida Nation.

A2.S2   The Haida Nation reserves the exclusive right to determine additional Haida Citizenship through a formal process accepted by the Haida Nation.

ARTICLE 3 RIGHTS AND FREEDOMS

A3.S1   Collective Haida Rights:

(a)   The Haida Nation collectively holds Hereditary and Aboriginal Title and Rights to Haida Territories.

(b)   The Haida Nation collectively holds Cultural and Intellectual property rights of the Haida Nation and will protect the integrity of same.

A3.S2   Individual Rights:

(a)   Every Haida Citizen has a right of access to all Haida Gwaii resources for cultural reasons, and for food, or commerce consistent with the Laws of Nature, as reflected in the Laws of the Haida Nation.

(b)   Every Haida Citizen has the freedom to remain, enter, or leave the Territories of the Haida Nation.

(c)   Every Haida Citizen has the right to hold other Citizenship as they choose.

(d)   Every Haida Citizen has the right of conscience, religion, thought, belief, opinion, expression, association, and privacy.

(e)   The official languages to the Haida Nation shall be Haida and English.

(f)   Every Haida Citizen shall have access to all public records of CHN except in the case of someone found to be guilty of or suspected of treasonous acts, in which case, he/she will be informed of the reason for denying access.

(g)   No Natural born Haida Citizen can have their Haida Citizenship taken from them.

ARTICLE 4 HAIDA CITIZEN PARTICIPATION

A4.S1   Any voting eligible Haida Citizen may propose policy legislation and vote to determine whether or not it is adopted, at the House of Assembly.

A4.S2   The voting Haida Citizens of the Nation will elect Representatives to the CHN, pursuant to CHN Election Procedures.

A4.S3   Any Haida Citizen may attend and participate in CHN meetings, and will be subject to the CHN Rules of Order.

A4.S4   The decisions of the voting Haida Citizens of the Haida Nation, at a House of Assembly will be binding upon the CHN.

A4.S5   Haida Citizens may through constituted means, recall any or all members of the elected CHN.

A.4.S6   All International Agreements, which go beyond the Mandate as laid out in Article 8, must be ratified by at least ¾ of the votes cast by a referendum vote of eligible voting Haida Citizens.

A4.S7   Consenting Haida Citizens may receive an appointment from CHN for specific tasks. Citizens may have such appointment rescinded by CHN.

A4.S8   Voting Haida Citizens are persons of Haida Ancestry who are 16 years of age or older on the day of voting.

ARTICLE 5 HAIDA CITIZENSHIP BY ACQUISITION

A5.S1   Adoption of persons not of Haida Ancestry by Haida families does not confer Haida hereditary or aboriginal rights to the land or right to citizenship of the Haida Nation.

A5.S2   No external government or judiciary may impose rights of Haida Citizenship to an individual who is not entitled by Haida ancestry.

A5.S3   "Citizen of Haida Gwaii" is an honorary designation, which may be conferred to a person who is not of Haida Ancestry. Such bestowal shall not be construed as granting of Haida Citizenship or Haida Hereditary or Aboriginal Rights.

ARTICLE 6 THE HOUSE OF ASSEMBLY

A6.S1   The lawmaking authority of the Nation shall be vested in the House of Assembly.

A6.S2   Resolutions and motions at the House of Assembly will be valid with the approval of ¾ of the votes cast.

A6.S3   The House of Assembly may establish Tribunals of exclusive jurisdiction.

A6.S4   The House of Assembly will be held the second week of October of each year.

A6.S5   Additional sittings of the House of Assembly may be held throughout the year with twenty (20) days notice given by CHN.

A6.S6   Annual House of Assemblies shall alternate between Skidegate and Old Massett.

A6.S7   The quorum of the House of Assembly shall be forty (40) voting eligible Haida Citizens. Such number shall be confirmed present by the presiding Assembly Chair prior to any votes being made.

A6.S8   House of Assemblies shall be called by the Vice President of the Haida Nation, or CHN designate, with twenty (20) days public notice.

A6.S9   The Vice President of the Haida Nation or CHN designate shall ensure the house of Assembly is audio and written recorded.

A.6.S10   The CHN Administrative staff and CHN Representatives shall assist the Vice President of the Haida Nation in implementing the convening of a HOA.

A.6.S11   By petition and signature, submitted to CHN, one hundred (100) voting eligible Haida citizens may call for a Special House of Assembly. The Vice President of the Haida Nation shall call and implement this House of Assembly no later than thirty (30) days of receiving the petition.

      (a)   Hereditary Chiefs' Council determines whether there are grounds for holding a Special House of Assembly.

      (b)   Special House of Assembly Agendas will only deal with the items brought forward in the petition; and to be signed off by the Vice President of the Haida Nation.

      (c)   Petitions will be reviewed based on existing CHN/HTS approved policies, procedures and regulations.

A.6.S12   The President; Vice President; and the CHN Massett, Skidegate, Vancouver and Prince Rupert Representatives shall attend and participate at all House of Assemblies.

ARTICLE 7 COUNCIL OF THE HAIDA NATION

A.7.S1   The Governing Power of the Haida Nation shall be vested in the Council of the Haida Nation (CHN).

A.7.S2   The CHN shall be elected by the voting Citizens of the Haida Nation.

A.7.S3   The CHN shall consist of the President and the Vice President, and four (4) Regional Representatives each of Massett and Skidegate, Four (4) Regional Representatives proportionately distributed to off-Island Regional Councils, and one appointment by each of the Village Councils of Old Massett and Skidegate.

As amended at the
2010 House of Assembly
                                        4
                        _____
                        President
                        Council of the Haida Nation

    (a)   Elected CHN Representatives may not hold an elected position on a Village Council.

    (b)   The terms of office are three years.

A.7.S4   The CHN will develop and enact policies pursuant to legislation adopted at the House of Assembly and in accordance with this Constitution.

A.7.S5   CHN Representatives will uphold the principles and dignity of the Haida Nation at all times.

A.7.S6   The CHN shall uphold the principles embodied in the Haida Accord enacted by Hereditary Chiefs, Council of the Haida Nation, Old Massett Village Council, Skidegate Band Council.

ARTICLE 8 MANDATE AND RESPONSIBILITIES OF THE COUNCIL OF THE HAIDA NATION

A.8.S1   The Mandate of the Council of the Haida Nation is Haida Gwaii and surrounding waters.

A.8.S2   CHN shall strive for the full independence, sovereignty, and self-sufficiency of the Haida Nation.

A.8.S3   CHN shall perpetuate Haida heritage and cultural identity, and will enact Policies for same.

A.8.S4   CHN shall protect the Domestic and Foreign interests of the Haida Nation and Territories through long-term strategies, negotiations, and steps consistent with the objectives of the Haida Nation.

A.8.S5   CHN shall promote a peaceful co-existence with other people and governments without compromise to the objectives of the Haida Nation.

A.8.S6   CHN shall establish land and resource policies consistent with nature's ability to produce. The Policies will be applicable to all users of the Territories.

A.8.S7   CHN shall regulate access to resources by Citizens of the Haida Nation and other users of Haida Gwaii.

    (a)   CHN through open and transparent consultation will develop processes that will be implemented for the use and the allocation of potential benefits derived from the resources of Haida Gwaii for the benefit of the Haida Nation.

A.8.S8 CHN shall conduct the external affairs of the Haida Nation.

A.8.S9 CHN shall provide for the Common Defense of the Haida Nation.

A.8.S10 CHN shall keep the Citizens of the Haida Nation fully informed and shall keep a Record of Proceedings, and from time to time publish reports on the activities of CHN, excepting such parts as may in their judgment, require confidentiality. CHN will publish "Haida Laas" as the official publication of the Haida Nation.

A.8.S11 CHN shall establish election procedures, which must be adopted by the House Assembly.

A.8.S12 CHN may delegate a consenting Haida Citizen to represent CHN on specific matters. Any Haida Citizen so delegated may have this responsibility rescinded by CHN.

A.8.S13 CHN shall maintain a Secretariat:

(a) The Secretariat shall be called "Secretariat of the Haida Nation." This Secretariat will include representatives of Council of the Haida Nation, Old Massett Village Council and Skidegate Band Council and the Hereditary Chiefs Council. The Secretariat will report to Council of the Haida Nation and to the House of Assembly.

(b) The Secretariat will administer the Haida Nation Treasury and Holdings and manage the programs and staff of the Haida Nation, as directed by the CHN.

(c) Pursuant to the Policies and Directive of the CHN, the Secretariat may:

(i) Borrow money on the credit of the Haida Nation with consent of the Council of the Haida Nation.

(ii) Regulate commerce with Foreign Nations and among domestic communities.

(iii) Coin money and regulate the value thereof.

(iv) Lay and collect Taxes, Duties, Imports and Excises, to pay the Debts and costs associated to supporting the Haida Governance; and provide for the general Welfare of the Haida Nation.

(v) Employ such persons or institutions deemed necessary by the CHN to carry out the CHN mandate.

A.8.S14   CHN may establish committees, institutions, and other processes to carry out the CHN mandate.

ARTICLE 9 COMPOSITION OF THE COUNCIL OF THE HAIDA NATION

A.9.S1   **The CHN Executive Representatives**

(a) The President of the Haida Nation

The President sits as the Chief Executive Officer and is the political leader and first speaker of the Haida Nation.

    (i)   The President is responsible to regulate the activities of CHN in a manner consistent with the Constitution of the Haida Nation.

    (ii)   The term of office of the President shall be three (3) years.

    (iii)   The President must be a natural born Citizen of the Haida Nation.

    (iv)   The President must reside on Haida Gwaii within sixty (60) days of election.

    (v)   The President shall take direction from the CHN.

    (vi)   The President, with consent of CHN, may appoint a specific portfolio to a CHN Representative. Through the same process, appointments may be rescinded.

    (vii)   The President, with consent of CHN, may appoint specific tasks to any consenting Haida Citizen. Through the same process, appointments may be rescinded.

(b)   The Vice President of the Haida Nation

The Vice President is the second speaker of the Haida Nation.

    (i)   The term of the office of the Vice President shall be three (3) years.

    (ii)   The Vice President must be a natural born Citizen of the Haida Nation.

    (iii)   The Vice President must reside on Haida Gwaii within sixty (60) days of an election.

(iv)   The Vice President shall take direction from CHN.

(v)   The Vice President shall call the sittings of CHN, and shall oversee CHN activities.

A.9.S2   Regional CHN Representatives:

(a)   The term of office of the CHN Regional Council Representatives shall be three (3) years.

(b)   CHN Regional Representatives must be natural born Citizens of the Haida Nation.

(c)   CHN Regional Representatives shall have one (1) vote on all matters in CHN requiring a vote.

(d)   The CHN Regional Councils shall be established and organized to represent Haida Citizens. CHN Regional Councils will form the base for consultation and participation between CHN and Haida Citizens.

(e)   Regional Council Elections shall be coordinated with general Elections of CHN.

(f)   CHN Regional Council Representation and structural organization shall be consistent with the Constitution of the Haida Nation.

A.9.S3   Executive Committee

(a)   The CHN shall establish an Executive Committee to conduct the affairs of CHN between regular sittings. This Committee shall be accountable to the full CHN.

(b)   The Executive Committee shall consist of one (1) CHN Representative from each of Massett and Skidegate, including the President and Vice President and will not exceed four (4) elected representatives.

A.9.S4   Departure of Council of the Haida Nation Representatives

In the case of departure of any CHN Representative due to resignation, disability, discharge, or loss of life, the CHN Election Regulations shall apply.

(a)   PRESIDENT: The powers and duties of the President will be passed to the Vice President forthwith.

(b)   VICE PRESIDENT: CHN shall, from among their numbers, select a new Vice President.

(c)   In the case of departure of both President and Vice President a House of Assembly will be convened by the CHN Representatives, and the House of Assembly shall decide which CHN Representatives will fill those seats, or may call a general election.

(d)   CHN Regional Representatives: An Alternate will fill the vacancy, or the CHN Regional Council may choose to have a by-election.

(e)   In the case of departure of any CHN Representative, positions of appointment may be recalled or re-appointed by CHN.

A.9.S5   **Limitations of Council of Haida Nation Members**

(a)   Any public representation must be consistent with adopted policy of the CHN.

(b)   Interpretations of CHN Policy shall be determined by ¾ vote of CHN quorum majority.

(c)   All CHN Representatives must act and be seen to be acting in the best interest of the Nation.

(d)   No Executive Member or CHN Regional Council Representative or person or entity engaged by CHN may use their position or privileged information acquired in the relationship with CHN for personal or other gain.

ARTICLE 10 SITTINGS OF THE COUNCIL OF THE HAIDA NATION

A.10.S1   Regular sittings of the CHN will be held quarterly, according to the seasons of the year.

A.10.S2   Special sittings may be called by written notice signed by the President or Vice President of the Haida Nation, or by the majority of the CHN, and at such sittings the CHN may transact any business and take any actions within its powers.

A.10.S3   At all sittings of the CHN, a quorum shall consist of eight (8) Representatives, no business shall be transacted unless there is a quorum.

A.10.S4   Whether assembled or not, a CHN quorum shall be able to transact any business or take any action within the powers of the CHN, provided that CHN has fully consulted each CHN Representative. Provision must be made for evidencing the concurrence of the quorum in writing, which shall be transmitted to the President for preservation in the Record of Proceedings.

A.10.S5   Forty (40) Haida, by petition to the Vice President of the Haida Nation or a quorum of CHN, may call a sitting of the CHN within fourteen (14) days of receipt of petition by the Vice President.

   a) The Hereditary Chiefs' Council will review petitions to determine whether there are grounds for holding a special sitting of the Council of the Haida Nation.

   b) Special sitting of the Council of the Haida Nation will only deal with the items brought forward in the petition; and will be signed by the Vice President of the Haida Nation.

   c) Petitions for a special sitting of CHN will be reviewed based on existing Council of the Haida Nation and the Secretariat of the Haida Nations' approved policies, procedures and regulations.

A.10.S6   Quarterly and regularly scheduled meetings, at which a quorum of CHN sits, shall be widely advertised to the Haida Public by the Vice President at least seven (7) days prior to the sitting.

A.10.S7   Each CHN Representative is entitled to cast one vote.

A.10.S8   All votes in CHN are recorded in the Record of Proceedings of CHN.

A.10.S9   Activities of the CHN will be decided by a majority vote of ¾.

ARTICLE 11 RECALL, REMOVAL, AND FORFEITURE

A.11.S1   Any Representative who, in the line of duty, is cited for neglect of duty, servitude, and public activity disrespectful to the dignity of office shall receive a notice of conduct from a ¾ majority of the CHN.

   (a)   The Hereditary Chiefs will be notified of all notice of conducts served.

   (b)   Decisions of conduct made by the CHN must be pursuant to the Haida Constitution; Haida Accord; HOA Legislation; and CHN Policies.

A.11.S2   CHN may issue a second notice of conduct, which may be a call for resignation or removal from CHN.

A.11.S3   Any petition for Recall, Removal, or Forfeiture shall be presented to the CHN and the Hereditary Chief's Council for review and may result in a notice of conduct or a call for resignation or removal from CHN.

    (a)   Any Petition must contain signatures of ¾ of last votes cast for the Representative, or 50 signatures, whichever is greater.

A.11.S4   Any Representative who is found to have used their position for personal or other gain, or who has acted in a manner deemed to warrant immediate action shall be asked to resign by a quorum of CHN.

A.11.S5   Any Representative removed from their position may appeal to the Judicial Tribunal.

A.11.S6   Any Representative who misses three (3) formal sittings without valid reason will be recalled.

ARTICLE 12   HEREDITARY CHIEF'S COUNCIL

A.12.S1   Heredity is an internal matter formalized through the ancient clan customs of the Haida Nation.

    (a)   The Haida Nation is a matrilineal society, and we recognize the prominent role of our hereditary matriarchs as part of our governing body.

A.12.S2   That only one Potlatched Chief from each clan will sit at the Hereditary Chief's Council.

A.12.S3   The Potlatched Hereditary Chiefs will assemble as the Hereditary Chief's Council to address the issues of the Haida Nation with provision of a recording secretary.

    (a)   An appointed spokesperson will be called by the Hereditary Chief to sit in his/her place, with written notice.

A.12.S4   The Hereditary Chief's Council will regulate its own activities through a process of a minimum of a ¾ majority.

A.12.S5   The Hereditary Chiefs will be notified of sittings of the CHN and will be requested to attend.

A.12.S6   Prior to a referendum vote by the Haida Nation, the Hereditary Chief's Council will approve or disapprove any International Agreement between the Haida Nation and other nations, which are directly related to Haida Title and Rights.

A.12.S7   The Hereditary Chief's Council shall uphold the principles embodied in the Haida Accord, an internal document of the Haida Nation, enacted by Hereditary Chiefs, Council of the Haida Nation, Old Massett Village Council, Skidegate Band Council.

ARTICLE 13 VILLAGE COUNCILS

A.13.S1   Old Massett Village Council and Skidegate Band Council perform the function of local government of their respective communities.

A.13.S2   Haida Village Councils are responsible for the well being of the Communities and will enact legal policies and programs for same.

A.13.S3   Village Council responsibilities include, but are not limited to, delivery of programs and services regarding cultural, social, education, health, economic, and municipal services.

A.13.S4   Village Councils shall each make an appointment of one of their Council Members to Council of the Haida Nation, and shall have the authority to recall said appointment with written notice to Council of the Haida Nation.

A.13.S5   Village Council Representatives will uphold the principles and dignity of the Haida Nation at all times.

A.13.S6   Village Council Representatives shall uphold the principles embodied in the Haida Accord enacted by Hereditary Chiefs, Council of the Haida Nation, Old Massett Village Council and Skidegate Band Council.

ARTICLE 14 JUDICIAL TRIBUNAL

A.14.S1   A Judicial Tribunal may be convened to resolve internal conflicts in a timely way.

A.14.S2   A Judicial Tribunal will be convened only when:

    (a)   All other Haida Nation processes have been exhausted to bring an issue to closure; and

    (b)   All parties agree, in writing, to accept and abide by the findings and ruling of the Tribunal.

A.14.S3   On consultation and agreement with the Hereditary Chief's Council and the Village Councils, CHN will select and appoint three (3) Haida Citizens to convene a Judicial Tribunal for a specific issue.

A.14.S4   Convened Judicial Tribunals will uphold the principles of the Haida Constitution and the Haida Accord.

A.14.S5   Hearings of Judicial Tribunals shall be open to Haida Citizens.

ARTICLE 15 INTERNATIONAL AGREEMENTS

A.15.S1   Amongst other strategies, CHN will pursue the goals of the Haida Nation through negotiations and diplomacy.

A.15.S2   CHN shall inform all Haida Citizens of all negotiations enacted.

A.15.S3   CHN will oversee the negotiation process and will provide the negotiators with the goals and objectives as well as ongoing direction and advice.

A.15.S4   Development of International Agreements shall proceed with full consultation of the Haida Citizens, Hereditary Chief's Council, and Village Councils.

A.15.S5   A final draft of any International Agreement must first be accepted by CHN and must then receive a minimum of ¾ approval of the Hereditary Chief's Council, and if so accepted, CHN will conduct a vote of the Haida Citizens consistent with the CHN Election Procedures and Referendum process of the Haida Nation. International Agreements must receive approval of a majority of at least ¾ of the votes cast.

A.15.S6   Signatories to International Agreement will be the President and Vice President of the Haida Nation and the Hereditary Chief's Council.

ARTICLE 16 RATIFICATION AND ADOPTION

A.16.S1   This Constitution must be adopted at the House of Assembly by ¾ majority**.**

A.16.S2   From the time of adoption this Constitution will be the basis of the Law of the Haida Nation.

A16.S3   The Constitution of the Haida Nation is the highest written law, reflecting the highest values of the Haida Nation, and any law that is inconsistent with the provisions of the Constitution is, to the extent of the inconsistency, of no force or effect.

ARTICLE 17 AMENDMENTS

A.17.S1   Amendments to the Constitution of the Haida Nation may be only at the House of Assembly by a ¾ majority of qualified voters present.

As amended at the
2010 House of Assembly   13
                         _____
                         President
                         Council of the Haida Nation

A.17.S2   Amendments may be made:

    (a)   For a ten (10) year period following the initial adoption of this Constitution at a House of Assembly, with a widely advertised two (2) month Notice of Change; and

    (b)   Thereafter, amendments to the Constitution will require four (4) public readings over a two (2) year period. Two (2) of these public readings must be at a House of Assembly. The other two (2) readings must be widely advertised as to their purpose at least one (1) month in advance.

IN WITNESS WHEREOF:

_____

Guujaaw, President
Council of the Haida Nation

_____

Date

APPENDIX 5:

Reconciliation Protocol

KUNST'AA GUU – KUNST'AAYAH RECONCILIATION PROTOCOL

Dated for reference _____, 2009.

BETWEEN:

> **HAIDA NATION,** as represented by the Council of the Haida Nation (**"Haida Nation"**)

AND:

> **HER MAJESTY THE QUEEN IN RIGHT OF THE PROVINCE OF BRITISH COLUMBIA** as represented by the Minister of Aboriginal Relations and Reconciliation ("**British Columbia**")

WHEREAS:

A.   The Parties hold differing views with regard to sovereignty, title, ownership and jurisdiction over Haida Gwaii, as set out below.

The Haida Nation asserts that:	British Columbia asserts that:
Haida Gwaii is Haida lands, including the waters and resources, subject to the rights, sovereignty, ownership, jurisdiction and collective Title of the Haida Nation who will manage Haida Gwaii in accordance with its laws, policies, customs and traditions.	Haida Gwaii is Crown land, subject to certain private rights or interests, and subject to the sovereignty of her Majesty the Queen and the legislative jurisdiction of the Parliament of Canada and the Legislature of the Province of British Columbia.

Notwithstanding and without prejudice to the aforesaid divergence of viewpoints, the Parties seek a more productive relationship and hereby choose a more respectful approach to co-existence by way of land and natural resource management on Haida Gwaii through shared decision-making and ultimately, a Reconciliation Agreement.

B.   This Protocol confirms an incremental step in a process of reconciliation of Haida and Crown titles.

C.   The Parties agree to focus on shared and joint decision-making respecting lands and natural resources on Haida Gwaii and other collaborative arrangements including socio-economic matters pertaining to children and families.

D.   The Parties agree that this Protocol represents the development of a new relationship between the Parties.

E.   Under this Protocol, the Parties will operate under their respective authorities and jurisdictions.

NOW THEREFORE THE PARTIES AGREE AS FOLLOWS:

1.   DEFINITIONS

1.1.   "Framework Agreement" means the Framework Agreement between the Haida Nation, Canada and British Columbia respecting the negotiation of the Reconciliation Agreement;

1.2.   "Haida Gwaii" means that portion of Haida Gwaii, also known as the Queen Charlotte Islands, identified on the map included in Schedule A, including the foreshore marine areas;

1.3.   "Minister" means the British Columbia minister, or designate, having responsibility for a matter in relation to this Protocol;

1.4.   "Parties" means the Haida Nation and British Columbia and "Party" means either one of them;

1.5.   "Protocol" means this Kunst'aa guu – Kunst'aayah Reconciliation Protocol between the Haida Nation and British Columbia including the schedules attached to it; and

1.6.   "Reconciliation Agreement" means the comprehensive agreement to be ratified at the conclusion of the negotiations under the Framework Agreement.

2. PURPOSE

2.1.   The purpose of this Protocol is to build upon the relationship between the Parties that will guide land and natural resource management on Haida Gwaii.

3. RECONCILIATION AGREEMENT NEGOTIATIONS

3.1.   The Parties agree to take an incremental approach to the negotiation of the Reconciliation Agreement as demonstrated by the implementation of this Protocol.

3.2.   The negotiation of the Reconciliation Agreement will be conducted using the negotiation process outlined in the Framework Agreement.

3.3.   The Parties acknowledge that a Reconciliation Agreement requires the participation of Canada and that both Parties will work to engage Canada's participation.

3.4.   Notwithstanding 3.3, the Parties will, in the absence of Canada's participation, continue to engage in bilateral discussions to achieve the purposes of this Protocol.

4. SCOPE

4.1.   This Protocol applies to Haida Gwaii.

4.2.   The Parties agree to address the following objectives:

  a)   shared and joint decision-making;

  b)   carbon offset and resource revenue sharing;

  c)   forest tenures and other economic opportunities; and

  d)   enhancement of Haida socio-economic well being.

4.3.   The implementation of the objectives set out in 4.2 will be in accordance with the schedules attached to this Agreement and future agreements between the Parties.

5. SOCIO-ECONOMIC WELLBEING

5.1.   The Parties are committed to an approach which recognizes and strengthens the interrelationship between environmental, social well-being and economic development, which includes but is not limited to children and families. A socio-economic approach, with children and families at the centre, will be developed by the Haida Nation with the engagement and support of British Columbia. Once mutually agreed upon, this approach will be jointly implemented by the Parties.

6. SHARED DECISION-MAKING

6.1.   The Parties are committed to working together in the interests of arriving at the best decisions regarding the management of lands and natural resources on Haida Gwaii.

6.2.   Schedule B of this Protocol sets out the framework for shared decision-making between the Parties for land and natural resource management on Haida Gwaii, including joint decision making where the Parties have provided the appropriate authority.

6.3.   Under this Protocol, the Parties will operate under their respective authorities and jurisdictions.

6.4.   The Minister will recommend to the Legislature, with the target being the spring 2010 legislative session, legislation to provide the statutory framework to assist in the implementation of this Protocol.

6.5.   The Haida Nation will recommend to the House of Assembly legislation to provide any necessary legal authority to assist in the implementation of this Protocol.

6.6.   The Parties, subject to signing a confidentiality agreement, will review each Party's draft legislation from the perspective of meeting the terms and objectives of this Protocol.

6.7.   In engaging in the shared and joint decision-making process set out in Schedule B, the Parties commit to make best efforts to seek consensus on matters addressed in that process.

6.8.   The Parties intend that implementation of the decision-making framework set out in Schedule B will constitute an incremental step in the reconciliation process through which legal rights and obligations respecting land and natural resource decision-making on Haida Gwaii can be addressed.

6.9.   The Parties will be responsible for the development, implementation, on-going review and refinements of the decision-making framework.

6.10. The Parties acknowledge that further refinement or amendment of Schedule B may be required from time to time to ensure that the authority, structure and functions for shared and joint decision-making meets the objectives of the Parties.

6.11. Further refinements to the shared and joint decision-making process and legislated authorities may be contained in the Reconciliation Agreement.

7. RESOURCE REVENUE AND CARBON OFFSET SHARING

7.1.   The Parties agree to share carbon offsets as set out in Schedule C.

7.2.   The Parties agree to pursue additional revenue sharing opportunities related to new major natural resource development projects that may be proposed within Haida Gwaii.

8. FOREST TENURES AND OTHER ECONOMIC OPPORTUNITIES

8.1   Forest tenure opportunities are set out in Schedule D.

8.2   The Parties agree to discuss other economic opportunities that may arise from time to time.

9. RESOURCING

9.1   The Parties agree that this Protocol is of mutual benefit, and the Parties agree to the principle that the cost of implementation should be jointly funded.

9.2   The Parties agree to implement the resourcing arrangements as set out in Schedule E.

10. AMENDMENT

10.1   This Protocol may be amended by the Parties.

10.2   Any amendments to this Protocol must be in writing and agreed to by the Parties.

11. DISPUTE RESOLUTION

11.1   The Parties are committed to resolving disputes that may arise in the implementation of this Protocol and may utilize dispute resolution mechanisms as agreed to by the Parties including mediation.

12. TERM

12.1   Subject to 13.1, the Protocol remains in effect unless it is terminated by one or both of the Parties.

12.2   The Parties will evaluate the progress and outcomes of this Protocol annually and will evaluate the status of necessary legislative amendments and implementation of the decision-making framework by July 2010, and based on this evaluation, may amend this Protocol.

13. TERMINATION

13.1   Either Party may terminate this Protocol by providing written notice to the other Party setting out the reasons for termination and the date on which it takes effect.

13.2   If a Party provides notice of termination under 13.1, the Parties will make reasonable efforts to resolve the dispute or issue, and commit to attending one meeting to explore the possibilities of resolving the issue. The Parties may seek the assistance or attendance of an independent mediator.

14. GENERAL PROVISIONS

14.1   This Protocol will not limit any position that either Party may take in future negotiations or legal proceedings.

14.2   Nothing in this Protocol fetters or limits, or shall be deemed to fetter or limit, the authority of either Party or their representatives

14.3   This Protocol is not a treaty or land claims agreement within the meaning of sections 25 and 35 of the *Constitution Act*, 1982.

14.4   This Protocol will be approved by:

a)   the President and Vice President of the Haida Nation signing this Protocol on behalf of the Council of the Haida Nation; and

b)   the Premier of British Columbia signing this Protocol on behalf of British Columbia.

IN WITNESS WHEREOF the Parties hereby execute this Protocol as of the date first written above

SIGNED ON BEHALF OF THE HAIDA NATION,
as represented by the Council of the Haida Nation:

ORIGINAL SIGNED

_____   _____
Guujaaw,   Witness
President, Council of the Haida Nation

and   _____
                                         Witness

_____   _____
Arnie Bellis,   Witness
Vice President, Council of the Haida Nation

                                         _____
                                         Witness

SIGNED ON BEHALF OF HER MAJESTY
THE QUEEN IN RIGHT OF THE PROVINCE
OF BRITISH COLUMBIA, as represented by the
Premier of British Columbia:

_____   _____
Honourable Gordon Campbell   Witness

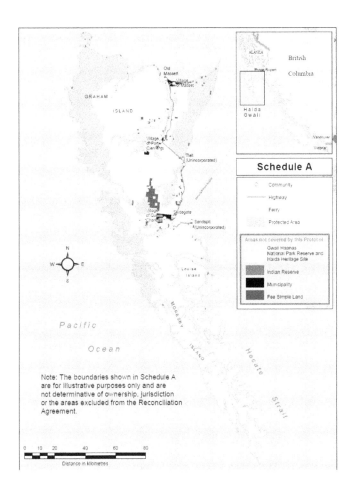

Note: The boundaries shown in Schedule A are for illustrative purposes only and are not determinative of ownership, jurisdiction or the areas excluded from the Reconciliation Agreement.

Schedule B: Decision-making Framework

The decision-making framework outlines a model for shared decision-making, including joint decision-making by the Haida Gwaii Management Council, for lands and natural resources that will assist the Parties in meeting their goals under the Reconciliation Protocol.

1.0   Responsibilities of the Parties

1.1   The Parties will be responsible for the development, implementation and on-going review of the decision-making framework, and may agree to make changes from time to time to that framework.

1.2   In accordance with paragraphs 6.4 and 6.5 of the Protocol, each Party will make recommendations regarding statutory amendments to enable the Haida Gwaii Management Council to exercise the authorities and functions identified in paragraph 2.2 and initially to enable the Parties to exercise joint decision-making.

1.3   Following the establishment of this decision-making framework, the Parties may recommend other authorities to be undertaken by the Haida Gwaii Management Council from time to time.

1.4   The Parties will ensure that their respective representatives in the decision-making processes will have the necessary authority to carry out their responsibilities.

1.5   The Parties will consider any matters that cannot be resolved at the level of the Haida Gwaii Management Council.

1.6   The Parties, in consultation with each other, will each appoint 2 members to the Haida Gwaii Management Council.

1.7   The Parties will jointly appoint the Chair of the Haida Gwaii Management Council.

2.0   The Haida Gwaii Management Council

2.1   The Haida Gwaii Management Council is accountable to the Parties for the decisions and actions taken pursuant to its authorities.

2.2   Subject to the approval of statutory amendments recommended by the Parties, the Haida Gwaii Management Council will be responsible for the following joint decisions:

      2.2.1   Implementation and amendment of the Haida Gwaii Strategic Land Use Agreement;

      2.2.2   Establishment, implementation and amendment of Land Use Objectives for forest practices;

      2.2.3   Determination and approval of the Allowable Annual Cut for Haida Gwaii;

      2.2.4   Approval of management plans for protected areas;

      2.2.5   Developing policies and standards for the identification and conservation of heritage sites; and

      2.2.6   Other strategic level management matters that the Parties delegate to the Haida Gwaii Management Council.

2.3   The Haida Gwaii Management Council has the following additional responsibilities:

      2.3.1   Development of a comprehensive Haida Gwaii forestry management strategy that maintains ecological integrity and supports a sustainable Haida Gwaii economy, for consideration by the Parties;

      2.3.2   Monitoring and review of the effectiveness of the Solutions Table;

      2.3.3   Identifying policy issues for consideration by the Parties; and

      2.3.4   Monitoring and evaluating the efficiency of its decisions at the operational level.

2.4   Decisions of the Haida Gwaii Management Council will be arrived at by consensus of the members, excluding the Chair.

2.5   Should the Council members not reach consensus, the decision will be made by a vote of the Council.

      2.5.1   Each member, but not the chair, of the Haida Gwaii Management Council will vote on all motions of the Council where consensus has not been achieved.

      2.5.2   The Chair of the Haida Gwaii Management Council will vote only when a vote of the Council results in a tie vote.

2.6   One Haida and one British Columbia representative to the Solutions Table will support the Haida Gwaii Management Council in a technical capacity.

3.0   Technical and Operational Level

3.1   The decision maker for each Party is the person authorized to make decisions on particular operational matters in relation to the Protocol.

3.2   There will be a Solutions Table which will be comprised of representatives of the Parties.

3.3   The Solutions Table is responsible for technical and operational matters including, but not limited to the following:

   3.3.1   Application of the decisions of the Haida Gwaii Management Council at the operational level;

   3.3.2   The review of applications, collection of information and conducting the necessary analysis to provide informed input to decision makers in accordance with the process to streamline the review of applications developed under 4.3.4; and

   3.3.3   Other matters agreed to by the Parties.

3.4   After receiving the input of the Solutions Table the decision makers may make a decision on the relevant application.

3.5   The Parties commit to further refine and develop the processes for operational level decision-making on Haida Gwaii.

4.0   Implementation

4.1   The Parties agree that decision-making in accordance with this framework will be implemented in a phased manner to allow the Parties to develop the processes and knowledge for effective shared and joint decision-making.

4.2   Within 4 months of the signing of the Protocol, the Parties will complete a decision-making framework implementation plan.

4.3   Items to be addressed in the decision-making framework implementation plan will include:

   4.3.1   A work plan and schedule setting out the application of the decision-making framework;

   4.3.2   Terms of Reference for the Haida Gwaii Management Council;

   4.3.3   Terms of Reference for the Solutions Table;

   4.3.4   Developing criteria and designing a streamlined process for review of applications that will include a category of applications that will proceed directly to the decision makers without additional review by the Solutions Table; and

   4.3.5   A schedule setting out milestones for the Parties to assess the effectiveness of the decision-making framework.

4.4.4   Completion of the implementation plan will be subject to the approval of the Parties.

Schedule C: Carbon Offsets

1. **Purpose:**   The Parties share the goals of:

    a. developing environmentally credible and marketable forest carbon offsets. These offsets would be associated with the additional sequestration and resulting greenhouse gas reductions from the creation of protected areas and changes to forestry practices ("Offsets") in the area identified in Schedule A;

    b. researching the eligible program criteria, the appropriate offset protocol, and the requirements for offset project plans. These research findings will inform the Parties of the potential standards for qualifying carbon reductions that could be converted to marketable Offsets; and

    c. entering into an "Offset Sharing Agreement" that would enable the Parties to share the Qualifying Offsets.

2. **Scope of Activities**: In order to build the framework for creating qualifying carbon reductions, the Parties recognize the following must be accomplished:

    a. identification of potential offset programs that may provide credibility and economic value to the Parties such as: the B.C. *Greenhouse Gas Reductions Target Act*; the Western Climate Initiative, Environment Canada's offset program, the Climate Action Registry, and any other offset programs that the Parties may agree upon ("Offset Programs");

    b. development, by August 31, 2010, of appropriate and credible models for estimating and proving long term projections of the additional carbon sequestration that will occur in the area identified in Schedule A as a result of new conservation measures and changes to forest practices;

    c. development, by August 31, 2010, of a protocol describing the technical basis and standards for the quantification of carbon reductions from the creation of protected areas and from changes to forest management which could be applicable in the area identified in Schedule A ("Carbon Protocol"). The Carbon Protocol will reflect the standards of, and be suitable for designation under, the B.C. *Greenhouse Gas Reductions Target Act* and any other agreed-upon offset programs, such as the Western Climate Initiative and the Climate Action Registry; and

    d. development of a process for validation or approval of a forests conservation project plan, or other documents, which:

      i. is appropriate for the B.C. *Greenhouse Gas Reductions Target Act*, and any agreed-upon Offset Programs;

     ii. is eligible for approval for quantifying specific carbon reductions; and

    iii. identifies who is responsible for carrying out the development, validation, and approval of a project plan or other documents and for paying the costs of these steps.

3. **Offset-Sharing Agreement:** Based on the results of completing the development work under section 2, the Parties will make best efforts to negotiate an Offsets Sharing Agreement by September 30, 2010.

    a. The Offsets Sharing Agreement will provide to the Parties a share of the total annual reductions from sources, sinks and reservoirs in the area identified in Schedule A that result from the carrying out of the conservation and changes to forest practices in that area ("Qualifying Offsets") for the purpose of allowing the Parties to have such offsets recognized under the chosen programs.

    b. The Agreement will set out how the total annual share of Qualifying Offsets will be distributed based on the following priorities:

        i. as first priority, a dedicated amount of each year's verified Qualifying Offsets, in tonnes, agreed to by the Parties to cover the cost to the Haida Nation of implementing, managing and administering the Offset Sharing Agreement;

       ii. as second priority, a dedicated amount of each year's verified Qualifying Offsets, in tonnes, to be agreed to by the Parties, to cover the remaining cost to the Haida Nation in meeting its obligations, under this Protocol, including management of protected areas, after utilizing any other revenues provided under the Protocol, excluding any revenues provided under Schedule D; and

      iii. as third priority, the Parties will each receive 50% of the remaining tonnes of each year's verified Qualifying Offsets, from the project.

4. **Other Matters**: The Agreement will contain provisions for:

    a. the review and monitoring of forest carbon data and models used to establish the quantum of Qualifying Offsets over the life of the Agreement;

b.   the ownership of the Qualifying Offsets or Offset rights and the legal form and transfer of Qualifying Offsets or Offset rights will be defined.

c.   the project, Offsets and agreements not creating any title or interest in land in the area identified in Schedule A;

d.   the project and ownership and legal characterization of Offsets not prejudicing positions the Parties may take on aboriginal rights and title or in Reconciliation Agreement negotiations;

e.   liability and managing risks of impermanence and reversals of Qualifying Offsets over time;

f.   the responsibilities for transaction costs associated with validation, verification, monitoring, marketing costs, and management of any Offset revenue;

g.   requirements that may enable Haida Nation participation in Pacific Carbon Trust procurement processes;

h.   periodic review of the implementation of the Agreement;

i.   dispute resolution; and

j.   any other components agreed to by the Parties.

The Parties agree to continue discussions on sharing of additional emission reduction opportunities for renewable energy and other environmental attributes that may arise from land use measures.

Schedule D: Forest Tenures

1. British Columbia reaffirms its 2005 commitment to provide a forest tenure of 120,000 cubic metres to the Haida Nation.

2. British Columbia will, subject to appropriations by the Legislature, and in accordance with the *Financial Administration Act,* provide to the Haida Nation, $10,000,000 for the purpose of forest tenure acquisition; this funding is an incremental payment of the total benefits to the Haida Nation available through the Reconciliation Agreement.

Schedule E: Resourcing

1. British Columbia will, subject to appropriations by the Legislature, and in accordance with the *Financial Administration Act* and any workplans and budgets agreed to by the Parties provide the Haida Nation with $600,000 per year to support the Haida Nation's implementation of this Protocol for a period of 5 years commencing April 1, 2010.

2. Upon signing of this Protocol by the Parties, British Columbia will, subject to appropriations by the Legislature, and in accordance with the *Financial Administration Act,* provide $200,000 to the Haida Nation to commence the Haida Nation's implementation of this Protocol.

3. The Haida Nation, subject to a successful implementation of Schedule C, will use portions of the resulting revenues to support the Haida Nation's implementation costs of this Protocol.

APPENDIX 6:

Mandate and Responsibilities of the Council of the Haida Nation

The official mandate and responsibilities of the CHN are found in the Constitution of the Haida Nation, which was adopted in 2003.

The Mandate of the Council of the Haida Nation is Haida Gwaii and surrounding waters.

The CHN shall strive for full independence, sovereignty and self-sufficiency of the Haida Nation.

The CHN shall perpetuate Haida heritage and cultural identity, and will enact Policies for same.

CHN shall protect the Domestic and Foreign interests of the Haida Nation and Territories through long-term strategies, negotiations, and steps consistent with the objectives of the Haida Nation.

CHN shall promote a peaceful co-existence with other people and governments without compromise to the objectives of the Haida Nation.

CHN shall establish land and resource policies consistent with nature's ability to produce. The Policies will be applicable to all users of the Territories.

CHN shall regulate access to resources by Citizens of the Haida Nation and other users of Haida Gwaii.

CHN shall conduct the external affairs of the Haida Nation.

CHN shall provide for the Common Defense of the Haida Nation.

CHN shall keep the Citizens of the Haida Nation fully informed and shall keep a Record of Proceedings, and from time to time publish reports on the activities of the CHN, excepting such parts as may, in their judgment, require confidentiality. CHN will publish Haida Laas as the official publication of the Haida Nation.

CHN shall establish Election Procedures, which must be adopted by the House of Assembly.

CHN may delegate a consenting Haida Citizen to represent CHN on specific matters. Any Haida Citizen so delegated may have this responsibility rescinded by CHN.

CHN shall maintain a Secretariat:

a) The Secretariat shall be called Secretariat of the Haida Nation. This Society will include representatives of Council of the Haida Nation and Old Massett Village Council and Skidegate Band Council. The Secretariat will report to Council of the Haida Nation, and to the House of Assembly.

b) The Secretariat will administer the Treasury and Holdings and manage the Secretariat of the Haida Nation Programs and staff of the Haida Nation, as directed by the CHN, through adopted CHN Policy and Procedures.

c) Pursuant to the Policies and Directive of the CHN, the Secretariat may:

- Borrow money on the credit of the Haida Nation with consent of the Council of the Haida Nation.
- Regulate commerce with Foreign Nations and among domestic communities.
- Coin money and regulate the value thereof.
- Lay and collect Taxes, Duties, Imports and Excises, to pay the Debts and costs associated to supporting the Haida Governance, and provide for the general Welfare of the Haida Nation.
- Employ such persons or institutions deemed necessary by the CHN to carry out the CHN mandate.
- CHN may establish committees, institutions, and other processes to carry out the CHN mandate 2013

APPENDIX 7:

Haida Claim of 2002

Action No. L020662
Vancouver Registry

IN THE SUPREME COURT OF BRITISH COLUMBIA

BETWEEN:

The COUNCIL OF THE HAIDA NATION and Guujaaw, suing on his own
behalf and on behalf of all members of the HAIDA NATION

PLAINTIFFS

AND:

HER MAJESTY THE QUEEN IN RIGHT OF THE PROVINCE OF BRITISH COLUMBIA
and THE ATTORNEY GENERAL OF CANADA

DEFENDANTS

STATEMENT OF CLAIM

1.   The Plaintiff, the Council of the Haida Nation, is the official governing body of the Haida
      Nation, pursuant to the Constitution of the Haida Nation, and is authorized to and does
      represent the Haida Nation.

2.   The Plaintiff, Guujaaw, is the elected President of the Haida Nation and is authorized
      pursuant to the Constitution of the Haida Nation to bring this Action.

3.   The Plaintiffs, together, represent the Haida Nation, including the Council of Hereditary
      Chiefs, and bring this Action on behalf of all citizens of the Haida Nation.

4.   The Haida Nation are Indigenous Peoples, whose territory relative to Canada's interests
      is Haida Gwaii, "Islands of the People", also known as the "Queen Charlotte Islands",
      which includes the land, inland waters, seabed, archipelagic waters, air space, and
      everything contained thereon and therein comprising Haida Gwaii (hereinafter called
      "Haida Gwaii"). Haida Gwaii is shown on a map, which is attached as Schedule "A" to
      the Writ of Summons.

5.   Without the consent of the Haida Nation, and contrary to the principles and accepted
      practices of the British Crown reflected in the *Royal Proclamation of 1763*, the British
      Crown claimed Title and the right to colonize Haida Gwaii.

6.   The Defendants are the successors to the British Crown.

223-00\00201

2

7.   The Defendant, The Attorney General of Canada ("Canada"), is the representative of
     Her Majesty the Queen in Right of Canada, pursuant to Section 23(1) of the *Crown
     Liability and Proceedings Act*, R.S.C. 1985, c. C-50, as amended.

8.   The Defendant, Her Majesty the Queen in Right of British Columbia (the "Province"),
     claims unencumbered Crown Title to Haida Gwaii contrary to Section 109 of the
     Constitution Act, 1867.

9.   Prior to and since 1846, Haida Gwaii was and continues to be occupied and possessed
     communally by the Haida Nation. Haida Gwaii is the homeland of the Haida Nation and
     at all material times the connection of the Haida Nation to Haida Gwaii has been of
     central significance to and the source of the distinctive culture of the Haida Nation.

10. Without limiting the generality of the foregoing, the Haida Nation exclusively occupied
     Haida Gwaii prior to and at 1846, by:

     a)   the continuance of Haida culture, which is based upon the relationship of Haida
          People to Haida Gwaii;

     b)   maintaining a spiritual relationship with the beings and the spirits of the earth, the
          forests, the sea and the sky;

     c)   living within and managing the human use of Haida Gwaii, and utilizing,
          conserving and protecting the terrestrial and marine ecosystems, to assure the
          well-being of present and future generations, in accordance with Haida customs,
          laws and traditions;

     d)   establishing trade relationships with other Indigenous Peoples, agents of nation
          states, and international trading entities; and

     e)   governing Haida Gwaii through the development and maintenance of institutions
          and laws related to lands and resources, including laws related to access and
          trespass.

11. Further, or in the alternative, in spite of the Defendants' disregard of the prior Title of
     the Haida Nation, and their efforts to control the resources of Haida Gwaii, the Haida
     Nation has maintained a substantial connection to Haida Gwaii to the present through:

     a)   continuing the activities and practices set out at paragraphs 10 a) to c) above;

3

b)   the exercise of political authority in asserting ownership of Haida Gwaii in dealings
     with other Indigenous Nations, the Defendants, and persons authorized by the
     Defendants to engage in industrial and other commercial activities on Haida Gwaii;
     and

c)   the maintenance and evolution of political institutions and laws, including the
     management of lands and the conduct of internal and external affairs.

12. The Haida Nation exercised, and to the extent possible, continues to the present to
     exercise the following practices, customs and traditions within Haida Gwaii, which were
     integral to their distinctive society prior to contact with Europeans:

     a)   used, harvested, managed and conserved fish and other aquatic species from the
          sea and the inland waters of Haida Gwaii for cultural, domestic and livelihood
          purposes;

     b)   used, harvested, managed and conserved trees, including old-growth cedar from
          the forested areas of Haida Gwaii for cultural, domestic and livelihood purposes;

     c)   developed a culture based upon the relationship of the Haida People to the land
          and the spirits of Haida Gwaii;

     d)   traded outside of the Haida Nation, fish and other aquatic species harvested from
          Haida Gwaii, for commercial purposes;

     e)   traded outside of the Haida Nation, material goods manufactured from trees
          harvested from Haida Gwaii, for commercial purposes; and

     f)   managed and conserved the terrestrial and marine ecosystems, in accordance
          with their customs, laws and traditions.

13. The Haida Nation has resisted colonization, and has been in an ongoing dispute with
     the Defendants over ownership and jurisdictional matters, especially matters related to
     the uses of the land and sea. At the same time, the Haida Nation has been ready,
     willing, and able to enter into good faith negotiations to reach an agreement for co-
     existence with the Defendants, particulars of which include the following:

     a)   the Haida Nation has formally served notice to the Defendants of the continued
          existence of Haida Title and Rights to Haida Gwaii, and remained open to seeking
          appropriate solutions which might harmonize Haida Title and Crown Title; and

4

b)   the Haida Nation has entered into the Comprehensive Claims Process and the British Columbia Treaty Process established by the Defendants, and other processes, with a desire to engage in honourable and effective negotiations.

14.   No Treaty has ever been concluded between the Crown and the Haida Nation at all, and in particular regarding, *inter alia*, lands, waters, airspace, resources, governance, or taxation.

15.   In the absence of any Treaty with the Haida Nation, and without regard to the Aboriginal Title and Rights of the Haida Nation, the Defendants have unlawfully occupied and exploited the resources of Haida Gwaii, and interfered with the Haida Nation's exercise and evolution of Haida laws, customs and traditions. In so doing, the Defendants have interfered with the culture and livelihood of the Haida Nation.

16.   Without limiting the generality of the foregoing, the Province has acted beyond its constitutional powers by assuming the right of exclusive control of Haida Gwaii and issuing exclusive tenures to lands and resources of Haida Gwaii and deriving royalties (stumpage, revenue and taxes) therefrom, without regard to the Aboriginal Title and Rights of the Haida Nation.

17.   The Defendants have trespassed and committed nuisance by issuing tenures which interfere with Haida occupation and enjoyment of Haida Gwaii and which have resulted in loss of biological diversity and caused degradation to terrestrial and marine ecosystems of Haida Gwaii. Without limiting the generality of the foregoing, the Defendants have:

(a)   appropriated for themselves or for their agents, land and resources of Haida Gwaii;

(b)   granted, replaced or renewed tenures to land and resources of Haida Gwaii to third parties;

(c)   collected royalties (stumpage, revenues and taxes) derived from the land and resources of Haida Gwaii, and prevented the Haida Nation from receiving benefits derived therefrom;

(d)   prevented, interfered or attempted to prevent and interfere with members of the Haida Nation accessing, using, harvesting, managing, conserving or protecting Haida Gwaii;

5

(e)   permitted the introduction of non-indigenous species of plants and animals to Haida Gwaii; and

(f)   failed to protect and sustainably manage the resources of Haida Gwaii, and in particular, the old-growth forests, watersheds and monumental cedar.

18.   Further, and in the alternative, the Defendants have infringed the Aboriginal Title and Rights of the Haida Nation by denying that the Haida Nation holds Aboriginal Title and Rights to Haida Gwaii and by taking the following steps:

a)   issued tenures, permits and licences to third parties within Haida Gwaii or otherwise managed and allocated lands, waters and resources of Haida Gwaii, in a manner which has interfered with the exclusive use and occupation of Haida Gwaii by the Haida Nation;

b)   conveyed land to itself and to third parties without regard to the Aboriginal Title and Rights of the Haida Nation;

c)   refused to properly consider and accommodate Haida Aboriginal Title and Rights in decisions the Defendants have made concerning the allocation of land and resources of Haida Gwaii;

d)   passed laws which confer discretion which is not structured to accommodate the Aboriginal Title and Rights of the Haida Nation to land and resources of Haida Gwaii;

e)   prevented, interfered or attempted to prevent and interfere with citizens of the Haida Nation accessing, using, harvesting, managing, conserving or protecting Haida Gwaii, and from receiving benefits derived from Aboriginal Title and Rights;

f)   collected royalties (stumpage, revenue and taxes) from Haida Gwaii; and

g)   failed to protect and sustainably manage the resources of Haida Gwaii, and in particular, the old-growth forests, watersheds and monumental cedar.

19.   Without limiting the generality of the foregoing, the Defendants have a constitutional fiduciary duty to consider Haida interests to Haida Gwaii and to consult and accommodate the Aboriginal Title and Rights of the Haida Nation prior to the issuance or renewal of tenures, permits and licences, and with respect to existing tenures, permits and licences for which no proper consultation has occurred prior to their

6

issuance.   The Defendants have refused or have failed to conduct good faith negotiations with the Plaintiffs to reach accommodation.

20.   As a result of the acts and omissions of the Defendants set out above, the Haida Nation has suffered damages and loss.

WHEREFORE THE PLAINTIFFS CLAIM as follows:

a)   A Declaration that the Haida Nation has Aboriginal Title and Rights to Haida Gwaii, within the meaning of Section 35 of the *Constitution Act, 1982*.

b)   A Declaration that Crown Title to Haida Gwaii is encumbered within the meaning of Section 109 of the *Constitution Act, 1867* by the Aboriginal Title of the Haida Nation.

c)   A Declaration that the Haida Nation is entitled to an Order for damages and compensation for the Defendants' unlawful conduct, as follows:

i)   compensation for unlawful occupation and appropriation of Haida Gwaii, and for infringement of Aboriginal Title and Rights;

ii)   damages in trespass for wrongful interference with Aboriginal Title; and

iii)   damages in nuisance for unlawful interference with the Haida Nation's use and enjoyment of Haida Gwaii and damage to Haida Gwaii.

d)   An Order quantifying the damages and compensation referred to above.

e)   A Declaration that the Defendants have unlawfully collected revenues from Haida Gwaii.

f)   An accounting of all profits, taxes, stumpage dues, royalties and other benefits in connection therewith acquired by the Defendants and/or their servants, agents or contractors in respect of Haida Gwaii.

223-00\00201

7

g)   An Order quashing such forestry, fisheries, mineral and other tenures, permits and licences which have been issued by the Defendants, without accommodation with the Haida Nation, particulars of which will follow.

h)   An Order of ejectment and for recovery of land from the Province for tenures issued by the Province which create ongoing damage and cannot be harmonized with Aboriginal Title of the Haida Nation, particulars of which will follow.

i)   All further and proper declarations, accounts, inquiries, orders and directions to carry out the remedies awarded.

j)   Interlocutory relief.

k)   Pre-judgment and post-judgment interest according to the *Court Order Interest Act*, and its predecessor legislation.

l)   Costs, including special costs or increased costs.

m)   Such further and other relief as this Honourable Court may deem just.

Place of Trial: Vancouver, B.C.

Dated this 14th day of November, 2002.

_____   _____
Louise Mandell, Q.C.   Joseph Arvay, Q.C.

_____
Terri-Lynn Williams-Davidson

Plaintiff's Address for Delivery:

MANDELL PINDER
Barristers and Solicitors
500 – 1080 Mainland Street
Vancouver, BC   V6B 2T4

Tel.:   (604) 681-4146

Fax: (604) 681-0959

Louise Mandell, Q.C.

223-00\00201

BIBLIOGRAPHY

Anaya, S.James. *Indigenous Peoples and International Law.* Oxford University Press, 1996.

Beck, Mary. *Heroes and Heroines: The Tlingit Haida Legend.* Alaska Northwestern Books, 1990.

Berger, Thomas. *A Long and Terrible Shadow.* Douglas & McIntyre, 1999.

Bial, Raymond. *The Haida.* Marshal Cavendish, 2001.

Blackman, Margaret. *During my Time.* Douglas & McIntyre, 1982.

Bringhurst, Robert. *A Story as Sharp as a Knife.* Douglas & McIntyre, 2009.

Cousteau, Jacques. *Islands at the Edge.* Douglas & McIntyre, 1984.

Dalzell, Kathleen, *The Queen Charlotte Islands. Vol 1 (1974-96).* Harbour, 1968.

Foster, Raven, Webber. *Let Right Be Done.* UBC Press, 2007.

Gray, Lynde. *First Nations 101.* Adaawx Publishers, 2011.

Gill, Ian. *Haida Gwaii.* Raincoast Books, 2009.

Gill, Ian. *All That We Say Is Ours,* Douglas & McIntyre, 2009.

Harris, Christie. *The Raven's Cry.* Douglas & McIntyre, 1992.

Howard, Bradley Reed. *Indigenous Peoples and the State.* Northern Illinois Press, 2003.

Jackson, Robert. *Sovereignty.* Polity Press, 2007.

King, David. *The Haida.* Marshall Cavendish, 2007.

Knafla & Westra. *Aboriginal Title and Indigenous Peoples.* UBC Press, 2010.

Lyons, Mohawk, Barreiro. *Basic Call to Consciousness.* Native Voices, 2005.

Penikett, Tony. *Reconciliation.* Douglas & McIntyre, 2006.

Saul, John Ralston. *The Comeback.* Viking, 2014.

Stearns, Mary Lee. *Haida Culture in Custody.* U. of Washington. 1981.

Takeda, Louise. *Islands' Spirit Rising.* UBC Press, 2015.

Thompson,Ruth. *The Rights of Indigenous Peoples in International Law.* U. of Sask, 1983.

Vaillant, John. *The Golden Spruce.* Vintage Canada, 2005.

Wilmer, Franke. *The Indigenous Voice in World Politics.* Sage, 1993.

Wilson, Jeremy. *Talk and Log: Wilderness Politics in British Columbia.* UBC Press, 1998.

Wright, Ronald. *Stolen Continents.* Houghton Mifflin, 1992.

ACKNOWLEDGMENTS

I HAVE so many people to thank for so many reasons. In no particular order, Jaune Evans, Claire Greensfelder, Guujaaw, Ian Gill, Jim Hart, David Beers, Terri-Lynne Williams, Tim Coulter, April Churchill, Louise Mandell, April White, Arnie Bellis, Gwaai Edenshaw, Diane Brown, Gwaliga Hart, Susan Musgrave, Thomas Berger, Armstrong Wiggins, John Vaillant, Rebecca Adamson, Douglas Higgins, Stacey Marple, Annabelle MacKenzie, Art Davidson, Colin Doane, Louise Mandell, Tony Penikett, John Wick, Harriet Barlow, Marion Weber, Phillip Frazer, Sophie Craighead, Siegfried Weissner, Tim Worth, Mary Zepernick, Wren Wirth, Josh Mailman, Evelyn Arce, Barbara Leff, and Arlene Singer.

And not to be forgotten are my brilliant editor, Jennifer Sahn, and Larry Levitsky, my guide through Inkshares. Also at Inkshares: Avalon Radys and Angela Melamud. And last but definitely not least, the ever-patient, stalwartly supportive Wenders… Love you, Dar.

I read about twenty books in my research. Two stand out. *All That We Say is Ours* by Ian Gill is a vivid narrative of the Haida's epic struggles against colonialism and for sovereignty. Although the Haida dislike the book (Gill knows this), it nevertheless provides a detailed and, I believe, accurate account of the islands' history. Accuracy doesn't seem to be the Haida's problem with the book. It has more to do with Gill's portrayal of Haida leaders and his sense of humor, which they clearly don't share. Gill was very generous with his assistance to this project, for which I am deeply grateful.

I am also grateful to Louise Takeda, whom I never met, but whose dissertation *Islands' Spirit Rising* provides a detailed tactic-by-tactic account of the Haida's strategy confrontations with government and industry.

Other books I relied upon are in the bibliography on page 251.

A word to my supporters: This book was pre-ordered and pre-funded by 373 reader/donors from around the world through my crowdfunded publisher, Inkshares. Your names are listed in the back of the book. My gratitude to each of you is eternal and unbounded, particularly the ninety-one of you who live within a short bicycle ride of my home and who put up half the funds raised.

This project was not funded by the Christensen Fund.

ABOUT THE AUTHOR

Mark Dowie recently retired from the University of California Graduate School of Journalism at Berkeley, where he taught science, environmental reporting, and foreign correspondence. In his final year, he conducted a series of courses on China's environment. Previously, he was editor-at-large of *InterNation*, a transnational feature syndicate based in Paris, and before that a publisher and editor of *Mother Jones* magazine. He is the author of seven other books, including *CONSERVATION REFUGEES: The Hundred-Year Conflict between Global Conservation and Native Peoples* (MIT Press, 2011) and *LOSING GROUND: American Environmentalism at the Close of the Twentieth Century*, which was nominated for a 1995 Pulitzer Prize. He has also covered indigenous issues for *Guernica*, of which he is editor-at-large, and for *Orion* magazine, of which he is a contributing editor.

ABOUT THE ILLUSTRATOR

Sgaana Jaad (aka April White) received her bachelor of science degree in geology from the University of British Columbia. She has worked as a geologist in remote areas of the Canadian West, an experience which has been of assistance in developing the visual faculty essential to creating her works of art. Entirely self-taught, April's natural inclination stems from her roots in Haida Gwaii, where being an artist is an honored profession.

April White was born on Haida Gwaii, the Queen Charlotte Islands. Through her father, she is a direct descendant of the renowned Haida artist Charles Edenshaw, of the Eagle Clan.

LIST OF PATRONS

Adam Hochschild

Alan J. Mooers

Alexandra Rome

Alex Freemon

Allison K. Barlow

Alvin Duskin

Alvin Hirshen

Amber Lawson

Andrea Peacock

Andrew Carothers

Andrew Tolan

Andrew M. Magruder

Angela C. Waite

Anna Hawken

Anne C. Dowie

Ann Hagedorn

Abba St. Germaine

Ana Manoel

Anne Murphy

Anthony Kline

Anuradha Mittal

Arlene K. Singer

Art L. Davidson

Ashley P. Phinney

Barbara Jay

Barry I. Oringer

Barry Traub

Belle Adler

Ben Ciotti

Betty Medsger

Bill Kitteridge

Bing Gong

Blake Hallanan

Bob Kubik

Bonnie G. Clarke

Brian J. Keane

Bruce Burman

Bruce Mitchell

Bruce Mayers

Burr Heneman

Carla B. Steinberg

Carolyn Brooks

Caryn L. Aman

Charles C. Mann

Charles E. Glasser

Charles Piller

Cheryl Higgins

Christine Nielson

Christopher Magnuson

Christopher Mc Leod

Christopher Palmer

C.J. Hadley

Claire Cummings

Connie Berry

Constance Mery

Conyus L. Calhoun

Corey Goodman

C. Parsons

Craig E. McGarvey

Craig Merrilees

Cynthia Ohama

Dakota Whitney

David Brast

David V. Harris

David Morris

David E. Reese

David J. Warnimont

David Miller

David Olson

David Sheff

David W. Wakely

Debbie Melnyk

Deborah Begel

Deborah Hayden

Deirdre English

Denis A. Hayes

Deni Y. Bechard

Dennis E. Mc Dougal

De Witt Sage

Diana Cohn

Diana Dillaway

Diane A. Levy

Diarmid A. Campbell	George Rush
Donald Smith &	Gleb Raygorodetsky
Jane Michelson	Gregg McVicar
Donna Sheehan	Guy A. Lampard
Don Murphy	Haley Leslie Bole
Doree Friedman	Harlan C. Clifford
Doris Ober	Harold Hedelman
Doug Elliott	Harriet Barlow
Ed Vulliamy	Harrison Sheppard
Edwin Dobb	Hathaway Barry
Elizabeth Woodman	Harvey Glasser
Elizabeth A. Zarlengo	Heather Preston
Erik G. Hoffner	Herb Kutchins
Eugene P. Coyle	Hobart Wright
Evelyn Eisen	Hugh D. Fullerton
Everett D. Reese	Ian Gill
Francis R. Currie	Ilene Briggin
Frederick Smith	Isi Beller
Freya A. Horne	Jacqueline Sa
Gail A. Grynbaum Rn Ph D.	Jacques Leslie
Gary W. Ireland	James Grant
Geoffrey Bernstein	James H. Campe
Geoffrey Cowan	James Keough
George H. Clyde Jr	James Lino

James S. Britell

James W. Mc Cormick

Jamie Hysjulien

Jane Canning

Janeen Williams

Jane Stringer

Jane Swigart

Jason F. Berry

Jaune Evans

Jay Bryon

Jay Conner

J. Campbell

Jean Driscoll

Jeffrey Cohen

Jeffrey Felix

Jeffrey Frank

Jeffrey M. Gillenkirk

Jennifer A. Wallace

Jennifer Sahn

Jennifer Snyder

Jerard E. Tanner

Jeremy Thomas

Jerry I. Mander

Jerry L. Spivak

Joanne Dornan

John E. Mueller

John Grissim

John J. Berger

John H. Schwabacher

John Lott

John Schabacker

John S. Turner

John Vaillant

John V. Everett

John V. Levy

John Wick

John W. Passacantando

Jonah Raskin

Jon R. Carroll

Josh Mailman

Judith B. Shaw

Judith Ciani Smith

Judith Coburn

Justine Coopersmith

Kalia Kliban

Karen Osborne

Kathleen Kahn

Kathryn G. Sylva

Katie Kleinsasser

Kerry Tremain

Kevin Hughes

Kimberly Carter Gamble

Kim Chernin

Kim M. Toner

Kimmy K. Johnson

Kirk Marckwald

Kristina Flanagan

Kristine E. Brown

Larry Levitsky

Laurel L. Wroten

Lawrence Janns

Lelia W. Seidner

Linda Blair

Linda Remy

Linda Schacht

Lori Pottinger

Louise Riswold

Louise Rubacky

Lucinda Setnicka

Lynne Greene

Lynn Glaser

Lynn Ireland

Madeleine Buckingham

Marcy Darnovsky

Marianne Levitsky

Marion Webber

Mark Bachelder

Mark Bovair

Mark Hamilton

Mark H. Harris

Mark Hertsgaard

Mark & Claudia Ropers

Mark Schapiro

Marna G. Clarke

Marshall I. Soules

Marshall Livingston

Mary A. Douglas

Mary Ann Petro

Mary Ann Rosenthal

Mary Ellen

Mary K. Pierce

Mary W. Zepernick

Mathieu Huard

Michael Anderson

Michael J. Herz

Michael Krasny

Michael L. Gale

Michael Nolan

Michael S. Archer

Michael Straus

Michael T. Klare

Mike Dillon

Mitchell Thomashow

Monica Moore

Nadia R. Sussman

Naneen Karraker

Nella R. Abbott

Nicholas Kline

Nieves,Evelyn

Nonnie Welch

Norm & Cheryl Slater

Norman Solomon

Patrick Dillon

Paul Blum

Paul Hawken

Paul F. Edwards

Paul H. Dixon

Paul Rosenblum

Peter Barnes

Peter C. Reynolds

Peter Buckley

Peter White

Phillip Frazer

Phyllis M. Faber

Rajeev C. Patel

Renee S. Yamagishi

Richard Charter

Richard Kirschman

Richard R. Olson

Rick Clogher

Roberta Suid

Robert Greene

Robert H. Schirmer

Robert Martin

Robert Kiesling

Robert Reich

Robert Simon

Robin Carpenter

Robin Turner Allen

Russell D. Chatham

Ruth Henrich

Sally K. Fairfax

Sarah Rolph

Sasha Abramsky

Scoby A. Zook

Sharon M. Jones

Sharon Helen Smith

Sho Campbell

S. Holly Stocking

Sir Zachary Slobig

S. K. Webster

Sheila O'Donnell

Sophie Craighead

Steven C. McKinney

Steven Friedman

Steven H. Katz

Sue L. Staehli

Susan Alexander

Susan A. Scott

Susan G. Allan

Susan Griffin

Susan Hall

Susan K. Fisher

Susan Sillins

Susan Sward

Sylvia M. Nogaki

Tess Elliott

Thomas Barlow

Thomas C Layton &
Gyongy Laky

Thomas Knudson

Thomas Silk

Tim & Wren Wirth

Timothy S. Kline

Todd Gitlin

Todd Oppenheimer

Tory Mudd

Troy Duster

Virginia B. Mudd

Vivienne Verdon Roe

Wallace Roberts

Walter Szalva

Wendy Schwartz

Whitney S. Gravel

William M. Dodd

William Shutkin

Yann Rousselot

Zoe F. Carter

INKSHARES

INKSHARES is a reader-driven publisher and producer based in Oakland, California. Our books are selected not by a group of editors, but by readers worldwide.

While we've published books by established writers like *Big Fish* author Daniel Wallace and *Star Wars: Rogue One* scribe Gary Whitta, our aim remains surfacing and developing the new author voices of tomorrow.

Previously unknown Inkshares authors have received starred reviews and been featured in *The New York Times*. Their books are on the front tables of Barnes & Noble and hundreds of independents nationwide, and many have been licensed by publishers in other major markets. They are also being adapted by Oscar-winning screenwriters at the biggest studios and networks.

Interested in making your own story a reality? Visit Inkshares. com to start your own project or find other great books.

Printed in the USA
CPSIA information can be obtained
at www.ICGtesting.com
JSHW022213140824
68134JS00018B/1026

9 781942 645559